W9-BSF-806

# Softball

# Softball

**SUSAN B. CRAIG**
Co-head Softball Coach
University of New Mexico
Albuquerque, New Mexico
Lifetime Member, National Fastpitch Coaches Association

**KENNETH D. JOHNSON**
Co-head Softball Coach
University of New Mexico
Albuquerque, New Mexico
Member, National Fastpitch Coaches Association

SERIES EDITOR
**SCOTT O. ROBERTS, PH.D.**
Department of Health, Physical Education, and Recreation
Texas Tech University
Lubbock, Texas

Brown & Benchmark
PUBLISHERS
Madison, WI  Dubuque  Guilford, CT  Chicago  Toronto London
Mexico City  Caracas  Buenos Aires  Madrid  Bogotá  Sydney

# McGraw-Hill

A Division of The **McGraw-Hill** Companies

## Book Team

Vice President and Publisher *James M. Smith*
Senior Acquisitions Editor *Vicki Malinee*
Developmental Editor *Sarah Reed*
Project Manager *Dana Peick*
Production Editor *Dottie Martin*
Designer *David Zielinski*
Manufacturing Manager *Betty Mueller*
Cover Photograph *Bill Leslie*
Series Photographer *James Crnkovich*

Basal Text   *10/12 Palatino*
Display Type   *Helvetica Condensed Bold*
Typesetting System   *Macintosh™ QuarkXPress™*
Paper Stock   *45# New Era Matte*
Production Services   *Top Graphics*

# Brown & Benchmark
PUBLISHERS

Executive Vice President and General Manager *Bob McLaughlin*
Vice President, Business Manager *Russ Domeyer*
Vice President of Production and New Media Development *Victoria Putman*
National Sales Manager *Phil Rudder*
National Telesales Director *John Finn*

Copyright © 1997 by The McGraw-Hill Companies, Inc.
All rights reserved

International Standard Book Number: 0-8151-1918-6

No part of this publication may be reproduced, stored in a retrieval
system, or transmitted, in any form or by any means, electronic,
mechanical, photocopying, recording, or otherwise, without the
prior written permission of the publisher.

Printed in the United States of America

10  9  8  7  6  5  4  3  2  1

# PREFACE

It is difficult to drive around any town in the United States without finding a park or a diamond where people are playing softball in the mild-weather seasons. From youth fields to adult slowpitch leagues to the newly formed women's professional league, softball has become a true American sport.

Softball may be played at a level where the players don't take the game seriously and are only on the field to have fun, but there are thousands of players who have a thirst for knowledge and want to learn how they can be the best that they can be. They want to solve the mystery of catching that sailing fly ball or reading the sharp ground ball that threatens to skip past the infield. *Softball* is designed to teach you effective techniques for play and drills to improve your game and to offer a solid understanding of the sport. Players must be students of the game if they are to master the exciting and challenging sport of softball.

## ▶ Audience

This text is designed for anyone who loves the game of softball and plays it, as well as for students in academic courses on softball. The book is intended to be an easy-to-read, useful tool that provides information about how to develop your game.

## ▶ Features

The information in this text can be used at any level of softball play because it contains basic rules and guidelines on everything from the mental and physical challenges of the sport to hitting drills. Chapter 1 details a brief history of the game and helps students to understand the current trends and governing organizations in the sport. Chapter 2 introduces the basic components of the game. The remaining chapters focus on the rules and terminology of the game, the facilities and equipment required of the sport, the basics of throwing, catching, hitting, and various approaches to game situations. Specific skills and drills are included throughout the book to help you increase your level of play. All directions in this book are given for right-handed players, unless otherwise noted.

In addition, this text offers special features that enhance its use:
- Each chapter has a bulleted list of objectives and a closing summary to reinforce the major points covered.
- Key terms are highlighted in boldface type and are also defined. This feature enables you to build a working vocabulary of concepts and principles necessary for beginning, developing, and maintaining your game.

- Performance Tip boxes outline techniques, applications, and strategies for quick reference.
- Assessments appear at the end of applicable chapters to assist you in evaluating your skill and game performance.
- The Appendix provides a game performance evaluation to help players evaluate their contribution to their team.
- Professional photographs illustrate proper techniques for effective softball play and complement the text discussion.

## ▶ Ancillaries

To facilitate use of this text in the classroom, a printed Test Bank of approximately 120 questions is available to instructors. These questions, ranging from true/false to brief-answer formats, allow for quick assessment of the basic rules and principles of softball.

## ▶ Acknowledgments

We would like to thank the following reviewers, who provided us with expert commentary during the development of this text:

**Emma S. Gibbons, Ph.D.**
Texas A&M University, College Station

**Bonnie J. Ferguson, M.S.**
University of Delaware, Newark

**Pat Lipira, Ed.D.**
Missouri Southern State College

**Bill Edwards, M.A.**
Hofstra University

We would also like to extend a special thanks to all past and present athletes at the University of New Mexico, who have shown commitment and dedication to our program and to our sport.

—Susan Craig
Ken Johnson

# CONTENTS

# Softball

# CHAPTER 1

## WHAT'S SOFTBALL ALL ABOUT?

## OBJECTIVES

*After reading this chapter, you should be able to do the following:*

- Give a basic history of the game of softball.
- Recognize the major organizations governing the sport.
- Understand current trends in softball.

## KEY TERMS

*While reading this chapter, you will become familiar with the following terms:*

- ► Amateur Softball Association (ASA)
- ► Diamond Ball
- ► International Olympic Committee (IOC)
- ► Kitten Ball
- ► Title IX
- ► Women's Professional Fastpitch League (WPF)

More than 40 million people from youth teams to senior adults play some version of softball, making it by far the number 1 participation sport in America. From the neighborhood sandlots to the minor league parks where the new **Women's Professional Fastpitch League (WPF)** plays to the **Amateur Softball Association's (ASA)** home stadium in Oklahoma City, softball is truly one of America's favorite sports.

From the time softball was first played in 1887, when it was designed as an alternative indoor sport, to the present game, which debuted in the Summer Olympic Games in 1996 in Atlanta, softball has a history that is as varied and complicated as the sport itself.

It started in November 1887 in Chicago inside the Farragut Boat Club. According to the National Softball Federation archives, it was there that some Harvard and Yale enthusiasts were awaiting the score of the football game between their schools. When a Yale alum learned of the Harvard victory, he picked up an old boxing glove and threw it at a Harvard alum, who tried to hit it with a stick. A game of sorts erupted, and George Hancock, a reporter for the Chicago Board of Trade, decided this was the ideal indoor baseball game. He tied together the laces of an old boxing glove, marked off a diamond on the Farragut Club floor, and put together a couple of teams. The Farragut team eventually challenged other area teams, and in the spring the game moved outdoors.

The game later moved to Minneapolis, where Louis Rober, a Minneapolis Fire Department officer looking for a recreational game for his idle firemen, adopted it. He marked off a diamond in a lot adjacent to a firehouse and used a bat that was two inches in diameter to hit a small-sized medicine ball. The game was soon adopted by other fire companies. When Rober transferred to another station, he called his team the Kittens, and **kitten ball** became the name for the sport until 1916.

Several names were used to describe the sport, including **diamond ball,** but the official name of softball didn't come about until 1926, when Walter Hakanson, a Denver YMCA official and a former ASA president, suggested it to the International Joint Rules Committee. The sport was not organized on a national basis until 1933, when Leo Fischer and Michael J. Pauley, Chicago sporting

In 1962 Joan Joyce pitched to Ted Williams, then considered one of the greatest hitters in baseball. He touched only 2 of 40 pitches, resulting in one solid hit and a foul ball.

goods salesmen, conceived the idea of organizing thousands of local and state teams into a national tournament. About 55 teams played in conjunction with the 1933 Chicago World's Fair in three classes: women, fastballers, and slowpitch. A 14-inch ball was used in a single-elimination format. In 1934 the National Recreation Congress membership expanded to include the ASA. The growth and popularity of softball since that time has been incredible.

The ASA has been the exclusive leader in the softball movement; however, some smaller organizations have cropped up mostly because of the emphasis on slow-pitch in the ASA. Organizations such as the American Fastpitch Association and the International Softball Congress both concentrate their efforts on fastpitch.

The women's movement brought some big changes for the sport of softball. In 1975 **Title IX** of the Education Amendments Act was passed, stating that institutions receiving federal funds must provide equal opportunities for men and women and that no one, on the basis of sex, may be denied participation in any educational program or activity. In the 1970s and 1980s, as Title IX started to have an impact, softball began to grow steadily on the college scene. Money began to flow into all women's college programs, and softball started to take off. The sport became one of the most popular team sports, drawing great crowds at the college world series. Powers such as UCLA and Arizona provided fans with action-packed games, and the ASA stadium provided the exciting environment.

The International Women's Professional Fastpitch Association (WPFA), founded in the mid-1970s, was the first attempt at a professional softball league. It was the brainchild of softball star Joan Joyce, golf legend Janie Blalock, and tennis great Billie Jean King. With recent successes in golf and tennis, these women felt that it was time for a new professional sport. The first league consisted of 10 teams in Arizona, New York (Buffalo), Illinois (Chicago), Connecticut, Michigan, Pennsylvania, and Southern California (San Diego, San Jose, Santa Ana). The first day of play was May 28, 1976. Unfortunately, financial problems plagued the league from the beginning, and the organization was shut down 4 years later.

▶ **Women's Professional Fastpitch League (WPF)**

New women's softball organization in which the players are paid to play a modified game of softball (smaller ball is used, base and pitching distances are farther apart, and base runner has lead off base.

▶ **Amateur Softball Association (ASA)**

The current governing body for amateur softball.

▶ **Kitten Ball**

The first unofficial name for the sport based on Louis Rober's team, the Kittens.

▶ **Diamond Ball**

One of the names used to describe the sport before the official name of softball was adopted in 1926. The term *diamond ball* was derived from the diamond-shaped field.

▶ **Title IX**

Legislation passed in 1975 as part of the Education Amendments Act that allows for equal participatory opportunities for men and women in any educational activity or program receiving federal assistance.

In 1989 the foundation of the second professional league started with John Horan, a college coach at Utah State, and one of his players, Jane Cowles. Unlike the first league, this one was the idea of an individual who was willing to spend the time researching what he thought would be a more fan-friendly game with more emphasis on offense. After Horan presented the idea to the Cowles family, Sage and John Cowles agreed to fund specific research on the game's potential. Horan wanted to modify the game by extending the field dimensions; by using a smaller, livelier ball; and by adding the leadoffs that made baseball an appealing running game. After some research and practice games in 1990, Horan established the National Fastpitch Association (NFA) in 1991 in Boulder, Colorado. By 1994 the NFA changed to the WPF and made an announcement of the first official tour in the summer of 1995, with the league beginning play in 1997 in eight cities.

Julie Smith's Dudley endorsement.

The acceptance of softball in 1992 by the **International Olympic Committee (IOC)** moved softball beyond the level of simply a recreational sport. This event has helped to increase respect for the sport, much like the explosion of gymnastics. The media started to take the sport more seriously with cable coverage of top National Collegiate Athletic Association (NCAA) Division I games and ASA major tournaments, and a second professional league with a different game started to make an impact.

Softball is a sport on the move. Although it has been a success story for many years, the popularity of college softball and the excitement of the 1996 Summer Olympic Games have brought the media attention to an all-time high. In the past men were asked to serve as representatives for some softball manufacturers, but the trend now is toward signing the top women fastpitch players to major endorsements for softball products. Lisa Fernandez, the popular star of the UCLA national champions, was the first big player to sign as she became the representative for Louisville. Two of the players now considered the best in the world and who played on the 1996 Olympic Softball Team, Dot Richardson and Julie Smith, signed major endorsement contracts with Rawlings and Dudley, respectively.

## Important Dates in Softball History

1887  The sport was first invented by George Hancock at Farragut Boat Club.

1926  The term *softball* was first given to the sport by Walter Hakanson to the International Joint Rules Committee.

1933  Softball was first organized nationally by Leo Fischer and Michael J. Pauley when 55 teams in three classes attended a tournament at the Chicago World's Fair.

1934  The Amateur Softball Association was adopted by the National Recreation Congress.

1975  The International Women's Professional Fastpitch Association was founded by Joan Joyce, Billie Jean King, and Janie Blalock.

1976-1980 Playing season for the International Women's Professional Fastpitch Association.

1989  The National Fastpitch Association (second professional women's league) was founded by John Horan of Utah State and the Cowles family.

1995  Name changed to Women's Professional Fastpitch League with its first exhibition tour in the Midwest.

1996  Softball made its debut in the Summer Olympic Games in Atlanta.

1997  The WPF has its first official season with eight teams.

## SUMMARY

- Softball started as an indoor sport in 1887 in Chicago at the Farragut Boat Club.
- The game was first called kitten ball, then diamond ball, before the game was finally named softball.
- Title IX had a substantial impact on the growth of softball, allowing women's softball leagues to gain enormous popularity and funding.
- The ASA is now the exclusive governing body in amateur softball that is recognized by the IOC in international competitions. It worked for the introduction of softball into the Summer Olympic Games in 1996.

▶ **International Olympic Committee (IOC)**
The governing organization of the Olympic Games that makes all decisions concerning the games.

# CHAPTER 2

# THE FACILITIES AND EQUIPMENT:
## VITAL TO THE GAME

## OBJECTIVES

*After reading this chapter, you should be able to do the following:*

- Have a simple understanding of the softball field.
- Describe the basic equipment required to play the game.
- Compare differences between slowpitch and fastpitch softball.

## KEY TERMS

*While reading this chapter, you will become familiar with the following terms:*

- ▶ Aluminum Bat
- ▶ Chest Protector
- ▶ Gloves
- ▶ Helmet

- ▶ Shin Guards
- ▶ Throat Latch
- ▶ Yellow Optic Ball

Softball is one of the most adaptable sports around. The facility can vary from a backstop in a city park to a major stadium. The game is designed to meet the needs of the players. The field dimensions are dictated by the age and level of the competition or the recent interest in making the game fan friendly.

# FIELD

A softball field is called a diamond. The playing field is the space within which the ball may be legally played and fielded. The field borders are marked by foul lines. The two major areas of the field are called the outfield (the grassy area in the deepest part of the field) and the infield (usually a dirt area where the bases are located). Home plate is the focus where the batter's box is located, with first, second, and third bases in order around the diamond configuration. Figure 2-1 shows a diagram of a typical softball field.

Table 2-1 demonstrates the differences in the field dimensions between adult and youth slowpitch and fastpitch games. It also reflects the basic differences in the rules of the two games. Pitching and bunting are the most important skills in fastpitch. Hitting is the foundation for slowpitch, so the distance to the outside fence is longer.

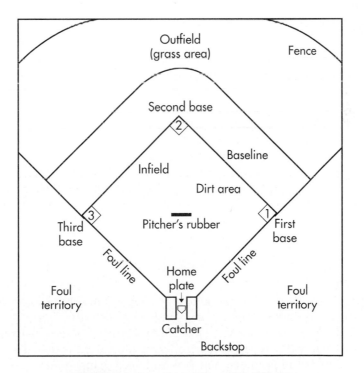

**FIGURE 2-1** Diagram of a softball field.

**TABLE 2-1**
**Field Comparison Table**

| | | Bases* (feet) | Pitching† (feet) | Minimum Fence (feet) | Maximum Fence (feet) |
|---|---|---|---|---|---|
| **Adult Division** | | | | | |
| Fastpitch | Women | 60 | 40 | 200 | 250 |
| | College | 60 | 43 | 190 | 230 |
| | WPF | 75 | 49 | 220 | 239 |
| | Men | 60 | 46 | 225 | 250 |
| Slowpitch | Women | 65 | 50 | 265 | 275 |
| | Men | 65 | 50 | 275 | 315 |
| **Youth Division** | | | | | |
| Fastpitch | Girls 10 & under | 55 | 35 | 150 | 175 |
| | Boys 10 & under | 55 | 35 | 150 | 175 |
| Slowpitch | Girls 16 & under | 65 | 50 | 225 | 250 |
| | Boys 16 & under | 65 | 50 | 275 | 300 |

*Distance between bases.
†Distance from the pitcher's mound to home plate.

In comparison to baseball, softball generally uses a smaller park. The pitcher's mound is level with the ground and not raised. In all leagues but the recent Women's Professional Fastpitch League (WPF), the regulation infield must be dirt, although recreation leagues may play on grass. The pitching distance can vary from 35 to 50 feet from youth ball to adult men's slowpitch. The recent WPF moved the women's fastpitch rubber back to 49 feet to encourage more offensive play. National Collegiate Athletic Association (NCAA) Division I colleges moved from the Amateur Softball Association (ASA) distance of 40 feet to 43 for the same reason.

The fence distance (distance from home plate to the fence) varies for the same reasons. The maximum fence in youth division is 175 feet but goes all the way up to 325 feet in the super slowpitch division. Throughout softball's history, the field has been studied, changed, and modified to meet the challenges of its participants or the needs of the organization that sponsors it.

# BALL

Although the baseball is 9 inches in circumference, the softball can vary from the 11 inch (used in youth ball and the new WPF league) to the 12 inch (in most fastpitch leagues) to the new 16 inch (in slowpitch). The NCAA recently adopted a **yellow optic softball** with a hard polycore on the grounds that the ball is easier to see and the harder ball will promote more hits and home runs. In most cases the ball is traditional white, although the cover may vary from a shiny day-night ball to a

**TABLE 2-2**
**Size of Typical Softball Bats**

|  | Length (inches) | Weight (ounces) |
|---|---|---|
| Fastpitch | 32 | 24 |
|  | 33 | 25 |
|  | 33 | 27 |
|  | 34 | 28 |
| Slowpitch | 32 | 27 |
|  | 33 | 28 |
|  | 34 | 28-36 |
|  | 36 | 28-36 |
| Youth | 27 | 19 |
|  | 28 | 22 |
|  | 30 | 23 |
|  | 31 | 24 |

rough more gray-colored day ball. Even the seams may vary from manufacturer to manufacturer. Pitchers are the first to test the seams to see if they are raised enough to allow for a better grip, which will help to put more movement on the ball.

# BAT

The sound of the wooden bat is a long-forgotten sound in softball. The trend has quickly gone to the more powerful, more durable, and much more expensive **aluminum bat.** As the sport has grown in popularity over the past 10 years, the selection of equipment has also grown. The length of the bat and its weight vary, as well as whether the handle is slim or fat. Some bats are evenly weighted, and some are end loaded (heavier on the fatter end of the bat). Even the grips on the handle are different. Table 2-2 shows the length and weights of typical bats.

Softball bats on the market today vary from wood to aluminum to titanium. Age and size of the hitter and whether the hitter is playing fastpitch or slowpitch are factors in selecting the right bat. Weights vary from 19 to 36 ounces.

▶ **Yellow Optic Ball**
Deviating from the traditional white softball, this is a harder, easier-to-see softball adopted by the NCAA. Since it has a harder core, it should be easier to get more hits and home runs with this ball.

▶ **Aluminum Bat**
A more powerful and durable bat than the traditional wooden bat, this type of bat is used exclusively today by the top players.

In fastpitch the weight and balance of the bat are key factors. Since reaction time is so short for most people, a lighter weight is usually better. On the other hand, in slowpitch there is a much longer reaction time, so longer and heavier bats can be used to increase the force generated by the swing.

To select a bat for a child, the size and strength of the child are very important. Children have a tendency to try the biggest bat they can find; however, what they need is a bat they can swing with little effort. The number one cause of poor fundamentals in young hitters comes from using a bat that is too heavy.

# UNIFORM

Each division has its own rules regarding uniforms, but basically any comfortable athletic clothing will do. As you go up the competitive ladder, the rules regarding uniformity apply; players are required to wear exactly the same uniform with numbers on the front and back for easy identification. In general, the choice between long pants and shorts is a team's preference, which may be based on climate or perceived appearance. Uniforms are bulky and loose to allow for easy movement. There was a time when baseball was noted for button-down jerseys and softball for the T-shirt style, but it is pretty much a mixed bag now.

## GLOVES

**Gloves** have changed from flat pieces of leather to well-sewn gloves specifically tailored for each position. There is a catcher's glove with a significant amount of padding to protect the hand from bruising. The first baseman's mitt is protected and longer to meet the needs of that position. An infielder's glove is generally smaller and has fingers that are about 12½ inches in length to allow the infielder to get the ball out of the glove quickly. The outfielder's glove is much longer, with finger length about 14 inches to allow for greater reach.

The batting glove was first used as a way to grip the bat better with the left hand. Now it is common to see hitters with a glove on both hands. Many defensive players wear a batting glove under their regular glove for added protection.

## SHOES

A shoe for every division, a shoe for every foot. From turf shoes that are popular in youth leagues to metal cleats worn in college fastpitch, there is a shoe for all players. There is no question that metal cleats provide the best grip for quicker cutting and better base running, but they have been outlawed in all youth divisions and in some city parks for both safety reasons and to keep constant use from tearing up fields and bases.

## SLIDING SHORTS

In most divisions of softball, players wear long pants because of the nature of sliding; in some areas, mostly in women's leagues, shorts are typical, and those who wear them usually also wear sliding shorts for protection. These are marketed by a number of companies and consist of a tight stretchy material that provides covering for the hip and upper thigh area of the slider.

## HATS

In most divisions the typical baseball hat is worn, but some women prefer the visor. Both serve the same purpose of shading the eyes and protecting the head from the heat.

## HELMET

All batters must wear a **helmet** to prevent head injuries. In youth ball an ear flap is required. Catchers also wear a modified helmet cap to protect the top of the head from foul tips.

## CATCHER'S GEAR

Because of the nature of the position, the catcher must wear a variety of gear to protect the body. A catcher's mask provides protection for the face; in many cases a **throat latch** is required to protect against balls deflected to the throat area. A **chest protector** and **shin guards** protect the catcher's chest and legs during the normal course of shifting and blocking and catching thrown balls.

▶ **Gloves**
Leather gloves and mitts that protect the hand. Gloves are specifically designed to meet the needs of each player's position.

▶ **Helmet**
Worn by the batter, this headpiece prevents head injuries from pitched balls. Many players choose a helmet with extra protection for the ear that faces the pitcher.

▶ **Throat Latch**
Part of the catcher's gear, the throat latch is worn across the throat to protect this area from fast pitches or deflected balls.

▶ **Chest Protector**
Worn by the catcher, this thick leather apparatus helps protect the chest from deflected balls.

▶ **Shin Guards**
Heavy pads worn by the catcher on his or her lower legs. This helps prevent injuries to the catcher when blocking pitches or blocking the plate against a sliding base runner.

## SUMMARY

- The softball diamond is one of the most adaptable of all sport facilities, changing to accommodate youth and adult teams, as well as slowpitch and fastpitch games.
- The basic equipment needed to play includes a ball, a bat, gloves, and catcher's gear.

# CHAPTER 3

## THE **RULES** AND **TERMINOLOGY** OF SOFTBALL

## OBJECTIVES

*After reading this chapter, you should be able to do the following:*

- Explain the basic rules of softball.
- Have a basic understanding of how to play the game.
- Know the basic responsibilities of each player on the team.
- Understand common softball terminology.

## KEY TERMS

*While reading this chapter, you will become familiar with the following terms:*

- ▶ Ball
- ▶ Bunting
- ▶ Fastpitch
- ▶ Run

- ▶ Seven-Inning Game
- ▶ Slowpitch
- ▶ Strike Zone
- ▶ Walk

The game of softball is one of the most exciting and complicated games in the country. On the surface, like baseball, it is a game that everyone can play; but for the student of the game it becomes a fascinating challenge that draws on many skills, both physical and mental, to be successful.

# PLAYER RESPONSIBILITIES

One of the interesting aspects of softball is its appeal to people with different skills. This is more evident in the fastpitch game than in slowpitch. On the defensive side there are eight distinctive positions to choose from, each with its own necessary skills: first base, second base, shortstop, third base, pitcher, catcher, outfield, and designated hitter (DH; does not play a defensive position).

In **fastpitch** the pitcher is the focal point. He or she must be prepared to handle a great deal of responsibility and credit for both wins and losses. To be successful, the pitcher must be confident and eager to meet all challenges. The first and third basemen must be risk takers and willing to play up tight to take away bunts while remaining alert to hard line drives. The middle infielders are known for their speed and finesse. Of all the players on the field, the infielders field the most ground balls. They must be dependable and good leaders. The catcher must be tough and able to withstand physical abuse from both blocking thrown balls and charging runners who are trying to score on a hit. Outfielders are known for their speed and strong arms, and they must be able to stay focused on the game even though few balls may come in their direction. Figure 3-1 shows fastpitch player positions.

In **slowpitch** the pitcher plays a lesser role in controlling the game but does more to contribute to the defense. The catcher does not need to worry about steals but still must shield home plate from players attempting to score. The additional infielder in slowpitch, called the short-fielder (or rover), is one of the most versatile players because he or she can play virtually anywhere the action is anticipated. Without a bunting game, the infielders concentrate on ground balls and covering their bases. Figure 3-2 shows slowpitch player positions.

# RULES

The rules of play are specifically laid out by the Amateur Softball Association (ASA), National Collegiate Athletic Association (NCAA), Women's Professional Fastpitch League (WPF), or any other governing body. Depending on the league, players should check local rules. Table 3-1 presents some general rules of fastpitch and slowpitch softball to give the starting player a better understanding of the game.

▶ **Fastpitch**
A version of softball played by 9 or 10 individuals (tenth player is on offense only). Players may bunt or steal. No arc is required on the pitch.

▶ **Slowpitch**
A version of softball played by 10 individuals with no bunting or stealing allowed. The pitched ball must have an arc between 6 and 12 feet high.

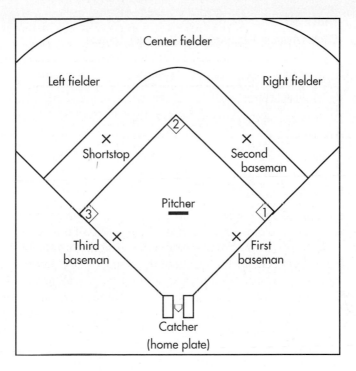

**FIGURE 3-1** Fastpitch player positions.

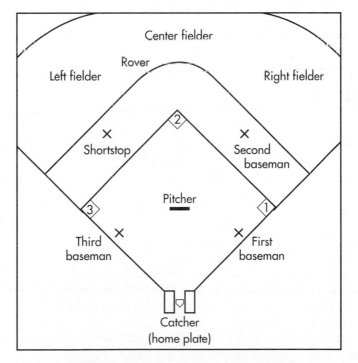

**FIGURE 3-2** Slowpitch player positions.

**TABLE 3-1**
**Comparison of Fastpitch and Slowpitch Games**

|  | Fastpitch | Slowpitch |
|---|---|---|
| Number of players | 9* | 10 |
| Innings | 7 | 7 |
| Steals | Yes | No |
| Bunting | Yes | No |
| Arc on pitch | None required | 6-12 ft |

*10 with designated hitter.

Softball is a **seven-inning game.** The home team plays defense first and bats last. The game starts when the pitcher, who must throw the ball underhanded, delivers the ball to the plate. The rectangular area that is formed from the batter's armpits to the top of his or her knees by the width of the home plate is known as the **strike zone.** It changes for each batter depending on their height. When a ball is pitched, the batter may decide to swing at the pitch or not. If the batter does not swing, the umpire decides if the pitch was a ball or strike. If the pitch is in the strike zone and the batter does not swing, it is ruled a strike. If the ball is outside the strike zone, it is considered a **ball.**

In softball each team is given three outs before they must return to defense. A **run** is counted when a runner completes the circuit traveling from first base to home plate. The object of the game is to move a runner from base to base before three outs are made and score as many times as possible. An inning is complete when both teams have had a turn at bat. The game is complete at the end of seven innings unless the score is tied. If this happens, the game continues until after a completed inning in which one team has scored more runs. An official game may be counted after only five innings if a game must be called for weather or darkness. Limitations may be placed on any game for time restrictions during tournaments.

In fastpitch if the batter gets three strikes, he or she gets an out. In either fastpitch or slowpitch four balls thrown by the pitcher allow the batter to take first base on a **walk.** In fastpitch the batter may hit an unlimited number of foul balls and still remain with only two strikes, but in slowpitch the number of foul balls may be limited to control the time it takes to complete a game. In fastpitch if the batter is struck by a pitched ball, the batter is awarded a walk to first base. In slowpitch a ball is called in this situation, but no base is awarded. If the batter swings and misses (at a pitch in the strike zone) or swings and makes contact with a ball that lands in foul territory, a strike is also called.

When hitting a pitch, a batter or base runner must reach first base safely before a throw is made to the defensive player on that base to be safe. The batter or base runner may stay on that base if it is a safe play, an error has been made on the play, or a defensive player decides to throw to another base and either doesn't make an out or doesn't make a third out.

The slowpitch game has some major differences since the pitcher must deliver the ball with a 6- to 12-foot arc and **bunting** is illegal. Because of the pitching rules, stealing is not allowed (as it would be very easy given the slow arcing pitch), and the additional defensive player (rover or short-fielder) is added to help cover the larger slowpitch field.

# GAME TERMINOLOGY

There are dozens of common softball terms that will be used throughout this text and throughout your years of softball play. These terms are important to help understand the game, the plays that are made, and the rulings that result. Following is a list of common terminology to assist you in beginning play.

**appeal play**  A play upon which an umpire cannot make a decision until requested to by a player or coach. The appeal must be made before the next pitch, legal or illegal. An example is a base runner not tagging a base as he or she passes it.

**arcing**  Term used to describe movement. Instead of moving in a direct line, a player arcs to be in a better position. EXAMPLE: On an extra base hit, a base runner arcs as she rounds first base to get a better angle to second.

**assist**  A fielding credit earned by a player who helps a teammate make a putout.

**backing up**  A fielder moving behind a teammate to be in position to stop the ball in case of an error.

**balance point**  The point in the pitching delivery in which the right hand is at its highest point above the head and the left foot is at its highest point above the ground. (FP)

**balk**  A pitcher starts his or her delivery but does not immediately throw the ball to the catcher. (FP)

**base hit**  Occurs when a batter hits safely without the aid of an error or fielder's choice.

**baseline**  An unmarked space, 6 feet wide, within which a runner must stay while running the bases. If the runner flagrantly moves outside this lane, the runner can be called out unless he or she is trying to avoid a fielder who is attempting to catch a batted ball.

**battery**  The pitcher and catcher.

FP = fastpitch; SP = slowpitch.

▶ **Seven-Inning Game**
The length of a softball game. An inning is completed when both teams get their at bats, and it concludes with three outs for each.

▶ **Strike Zone**
The rectangular area formed by the width of home plate by the distance from the batter's arm pits to his or her knees.

▶ **Ball**
The umpire's ruling of a pitch that is thrown outside of the strike zone and at which the batter does not swing.

▶ **Run**
A score for the team at bat, accomplished by completing the base circuit from first base to home plate before three outs occur.

▶ **Walk**
A walk to first base that is awarded to the batter if four balls are pitched.

▶ **Bunting (Fastpitch Only)**
Lightly tapping a pitch with the bat, sending the ball either down a foul line or in front of home plate. This is used to move base runners in better scoring position.

**beat out**  A batter hits a ball to an infielder and reaches first base before a play can be made.

**blooper**  A batted ball that flies over the infielder's head and falls in front of the outfielders for a base hit.

**bunt**  A ball tapped a <u>short distance</u> down either foul line or in front of home plate by a batter attempting to advance a base runner or achieve an infield hit. *(FP)*

**change-up**  A pitch intentionally thrown much slower than normal to keep the hitter off balance. (FP)

**choking up**  A grip in which the hitter moves his or her hands up the bat handle to increase bat control.

**cleanup**  The fourth position in the batting order, usually given to a power hitter.

**cock**  The action in which a pitcher holds the throwing hand at a right angle to the forearm in preparation for the wrist snap.

**count**  The number of balls and strikes on a batter.

**corner players**  First and third basemen.

**covering the base**  Assuming a baseman's position and responsibilities at that base.

**crossover step**  An agility drill in which a runner runs down an imaginary line, crossing back and forth across this path.

**crow hop**  Using the body and arm in a throwing motion that generates maximum velocity on the ball.

**cut**  An infielder's interception of a throw from an outfielder or another infielder when no play can be made at the intended base or when another play is foreseen.

**delay steal**  An attempt to steal a base whereby the runner does not leave until the catcher releases the ball. (<u>FP</u>)

**designated hitter (DH)**  A hitter designated to bat for any one starting player in the game. (FP)

**do-or-die play (situation)**  An outfield technique used to field a ground ball on the run, enabling the outfielder to release the ball more quickly and produce more force behind it.

**double play**  A defensive maneuver resulting in two outs in one play.

**double steal**  Two runners attempt to steal bases on the same play.

**drag bunt**  A batter executes a bunt at the last possible second in an attempt to catch the infielders by surprise, resulting in a base hit.

**drifting**  Timing the flight of a fly ball with the movement of the body so that both will arrive at the same point simultaneously.

**drop step**  A defensive technique that allows the fielder to approach a ground or fly ball in the most efficient manner and gain depth on those balls hit away from the fielder.

**drop the hips**  Moving from a standing position to an athletic position by bending the knees and dropping the hips for a lower center of gravity.

**earned run**  A run that was scored through an offensive play rather than a defensive mistake.

**earned run average (ERA)**  The average number of earned runs that a pitcher allows during a full game. To determine the ERA, multiply the number of earned runs allowed by seven, then divide by total innings pitched.

**error**  A misplayed ball.

**fair ball**  A batted ball that is touched or stops in the field between the foul lines or that initially lands between the foul lines and beyond the bases.

**fake bunt**  Assuming a bunting stance without attempting to bunt the ball. Primarily used to draw the basemen in close and away from their base-covering assignments. (FP)

**fartlek**  A form of training designed primarily as a conditioning modality that combines slow jogging intervals with sprint intervals.

**fielder's choice**  A play in which a fielder attempts to put out one runner, allowing another runner or runners to advance safely.

**force-out**  A putout on a base runner who had to advance because the batter becomes a base runner.

**foul ball**  A batted ball that is touched or stops outside the foul lines between home plate and first or third base, that bounces past first or third base in foul territory, or that first lands outside the foul lines on a fly past first or third base.

**full count**  A count of three balls and two strikes on a batter.

**fungo**  A self-tossed hit.

**grand slam**  A home run with a runner at each base.

**grounder (ground ball)**  A batted ball on which no play is made before it hits or rolls on the ground.

**hit**  A legally batted ball that results in a batter successfully getting on base through no error by the defense.

**hit and run**  An offensive strategy in which the batter hits and the base runner steals on the pitch. (FP)

**hit batsman**  A batter who is hit by a pitched ball. The batter is entitled to move to first base. (FP)

**hitting behind the runner**  A batter intentionally hits the ball to an area behind the path of a runner.

**infield fly**  A fly ball hit in fair territory that can be easily caught by an infielder. With less than two outs and runners at first and second or first, second, and third, the batter is automatically out.

**inside-out swing**  When initiating the swing, the batter brings the hands into the body, allowing the batter to hit the ball over the plate.

**inside pitch**  Pitch that comes over the part of the plate closest to the batter.

**interference**  A hindrance by a player that prevents the defensive fielder from making a play.

**leadoff**  A quick move off the base taken by a base runner as soon as the ball leaves the pitcher's hand. (FP)

**line drive**  A batted ball hit on a plane parallel to the ground.

**middle infielders**  Second baseman and shortstop.

**obstruction**  An act of a fielder who, while not in possession of the ball or in the act of fielding a batted ball, impedes the progress of a base runner who is legally running bases.

**outside pitch**  Pitch that comes over that part of the plate farthest away from the batter.

**overrun**  To run or slide past a base. The batter may overrun first base without being tagged out as long as the runner makes no attempt to advance to second.

**passed ball**  A legally pitched ball that the catcher fails to hold and control and that the bat did not strike. (FP)

**pickoff**  A play to trap a runner off base with a sudden throw and tag for an out. (FP)

**pinch hitter**  A player who is sent into a game to bat in place of another batter.

**pinch runner**  A player who is sent into a game to run for a player who has reached base.

**pitchout** A defensive tactic in which the pitcher intentionally throws a pitch wide of the plate to allow the catcher to field the ball quickly for a possible play on a base runner. (FP)

**power point** The spot in the pitching delivery at which the perfect timing between the wrist and hip snap results in maximal force on the ball. (FP)

**premotion** A natural motion executed by a pitcher to prepare for the delivery. (FP)

**putout** A scoring term giving credit to the defensive player who catches a fly ball or throws someone out after a ground ball.

**quick throw** A technique used by infielders to remove a ball from the glove as quickly as possible.

**relay** To return the ball from the outfield to the infield by using several short, quick throws rather than one long one.

**rundown** A situation that arises when a base runner is caught between two bases.

**runs batted in (RBI)** If a base runner scores when a batter gets a base hit, sacrifices, forces in a run by being walked, or hits into a putout, the batter is credited with batting in a run.

**sacrifice** Advancement of a base runner by a batter who deliberately hits the ball in such a way that the defensive fielders can only make a play on the hitter.

**short-fielder (rover)** A tenth defensive player who can be placed anywhere; usually becomes a fourth outfielder. (SP)

**shut out** To prevent the opposing team from scoring a run.

**6-12 rotation** A top spin applied to the ball during an overhand throw.

**slap bunt** A bunt technique used by both left- and right-handed batters to slap the ball by in-rushing corner players.

**slingshot** A pitching delivery in which the pitcher swings the throwing arm in an arc directly back and up to a point above the head before following through by the hip and releasing the ball.

**slow roller** Returns to the speed of a ground ball.

**snap throw** A throwing technique used to assure a quick and accurate throw over short distances.

**squeeze play** Scoring a runner from third base to home plate by bunting the ball. The base runner starts running as soon as the ball is pitched, and the batter must bunt the ball no matter where it is pitched.

**squeeze bunt** A bunt executed with a runner on third. On a given pitch, the runner attempts to steal home and the hitter bunts the ball.

**steal** To advance to another base on the strength of base running alone.

**pitcher's stride** The length of the step made by the pitcher's left foot. The distance should be no more than 4½ steps of the pitcher's own foot. (FP)

**supination** Rotation of the forearm and hand so that the palm faces forward or upward.

**soft hands** An infielder gives with the ground ball by relaxing the arms, hands, and fingers as the ball enters the glove.

**tag** When there is no force-out, the action of an infielder tagging a base runner with the ball.

**tagup** The action of a base runner touching a base while a fielder is catching a fly ball.

**trap** To catch a ball immediately after it has taken its first bounce.

**wild pitch** An inaccurately delivered pitch that the catcher has little or no chance of stopping or holding. (FP)

**windmill** A pitching delivery in which the pitcher makes a circle, starting in front of the body, swinging over the head, and ending just after the hand and arm pass the right hip. (FP)

**wrist snap** A snap of the wrist by a pitcher to put speed and movement on the ball. (FP)

## SUMMARY

- There are 8 distinctive defensive positions in fastpitch softball and 10 in slowpitch, each with different responsibilities.
- The pitching game defines the major differences between slowpitch and fastpitch games.
- A game of softball consists of seven innings.
- An inning is complete when both teams have had a turn at bat.

# CHAPTER 4

# HOW TO GET STARTED
## MENTALLY AND PHYSICALLY

## OBJECTIVES

*After reading this chapter, you should be able to do the following:*

- Understand the mental and physical challenges of the sport.
- Explain agility drills that can improve an individual's athletic performance.
- Describe some creative workouts that will both condition the athlete and help improve basic game skills.
- Have an idea of what must be done in pregame warm-ups.
- Describe a stretching routine to keep an athlete fit and help prevent injuries.

## KEY TERMS

*While reading this chapter, you will become familiar with the following terms:*

▶ Agility Drills ▶ Stretching
▶ Conditioning ▶ Weight Training

As with any sport, a consistent warm-up pattern is needed to prepare the athlete mentally and physically for the game. Whether it be in a physical education class or an official tournament game, preparation enhances performance, prevents injuries, and makes the game more enjoyable.

## MENTAL PREPARATION

Sport psychologists confirm that softball is one of the most difficult games in which to maintain concentration because it is not a game of continuous action. Like a roller-coaster rider, a softball player must deal with sudden and emotion-packed action followed by quiet moments that tempt the player to relax too much and lose focus. An outfielder may not field a fly ball for three innings and then suddenly see a ball driven toward the fence, requiring an immediate reaction. A hitter may sit in the dugout for two innings before coming to bat. In a short period of time the hitter must regenerate the emotion, focus, and aggression needed to be a successful hitter.

As with physical skills, each individual player must understand what it takes for he or she to be successful. There is no quick-fix formula for every player. Some prefer to be quiet, and others become very animated during the game. Talking helps some people stay focused, but silent concentration works for others. The key is keeping the mind focused on the game at hand and not allowing outside distractions to break the fragile concentration.

## STRETCHING

**Stretching** plays a vital role in the physical and mental well-being of any athlete but increases in importance as the athlete ages. A good stretching program increases flexibility and helps to keep the muscles from getting tense and tight during and after play. A consistent program of stretching can help anyone relax.

One of the top books on the market is simply called *Stretching* by Jean and Bob Anderson (Shelter Publications, 1980). Although the book was first published in 1975, it is still considered by many the primary source for reliable information. According to the Andersons, stretching is the foundation of movement, and they recommend that all stretches be held from 30 to 60 seconds to gain the most benefit.

In their book the Andersons detail a series of stretching exercises for a variety of sports including baseball. This 30-minute routine works all the essential muscles used in the sport including the hamstrings, quadriceps, back, biceps, triceps, pectorals, and the fingers, hands, wrists and forearms. When creating a program for the individual, each player should consult this book and talk to other respected experts in the field.

▶ **Stretching**
  Working the muscles to make them more flexible, which results in fewer injuries during play.

# CONDITIONING

**Conditioning** can be the single most dreaded word in any athlete's vocabulary. It was originally used to simply mean running until you drop and naturally was not the most popular part of any practice. But times have changed, and conditioning has become more sophisticated. Because coaches are getting more creative and because it conserves time, conditioning is now a normal part of everyday practice that teaches skills while getting athletes in shape. One of the obvious ways of helping athletes get into shape is by improving the attitude they carry into practice or class.

By simply working hard at every skill an athlete is attempting conditioning. As long as there is a work ethic, doing skills every day can condition and strengthen any player. Taking 100 swings a day in various drills builds strength. Taking ground balls for 10 minutes conditions any athlete and builds strong legs. Chasing down fly balls for 20 minutes builds running skills. Practicing base running helps anyone. If an athlete makes a commitment to the sport and gives 100% each day to improving, conditioning is not a chore but another way of becoming a better player.

Conditioning is not just a way to improve skills but also allows the well-conditioned athlete to perform better for longer periods of time than players who don't commit to getting into shape. Also, being in shape helps players avoid injuries since many injuries are caused by fatigue or lack of flexibility. In the new sense conditioning is not just dull work; it is training that teaches athletes to execute fundamentals correctly even when tired. Fatigue affects concentration, so the body must be in shape to overcome lapses of the mind.

# CONFIDENCE THROUGH BODY AWARENESS

It only makes sense that an athlete who has confidence in controlling his or her own body has more confidence in handling other skills. An awkward athlete who has no sense of balance or body control has good reason to doubt his or her ability to master basic skills like throwing and catching. **Agility drills** are one of the best ways to teach anyone about his or her body. Putting a player through a series of tasks that call for quick turning, jumping, and changing directions teaches body control and awareness. Agility drills are about footwork and balance. Some drills used to help with conditioning are explained in the chapter assessment. In addition, the five drills that follow are ones that every softball player should practice to help improve or perfect the basic moves required by the sport.

## KARIOKA

A player stands on the right field line facing center field. Using a grapevine step, the player moves down the line toward the foul pole with the left leg crossing first in front and then in back of the right foot, twisting the hips back and forth. The trunk must stay parallel to the foul line. By facing the same direction on the way back, the player uses the opposite foot when crossing over. This teaches fast, effective footwork. Figures 4-1 through 4-4 demonstrate this drill.

**FIGURE 4-1** Player beginning the karioka drill. Body is parallel to the foul line. Shoulders are square.

**FIGURE 4-2** Player begins to move right, crossing the left leg in front of the right leg.

**FIGURE 4-3** Player steps out with the right leg. Hips are facing forward.

**FIGURE 4-4** Left leg crosses behind right leg. Player reverses direction and moves back to the left, crossing right leg in front of and behind left leg.

▶ **Conditioning**
The process of increasing the athlete's fitness level through practice of the fundamental skills and strength exercises.

▶ **Agility Drills**
Drills to help quicken the athlete's footwork and perfect his or her balance, which will inevitably help improve the basic skills required of the sport.

# JUMP TURN

A player runs at full speed (or can begin in a ready position), jumps straight up, extending the arms upward, turning 180 degrees, landing on the feet with a wide base, dropping the hips, and bringing the hands down to the chest level. The weight must end up centered over the hips to allow the athlete to land in control of his or her body and with the ability to move in any direction. Figures 4-5 through 4-8 illustrate the correct progression of this drill.

**FIGURE 4-5** Ready position for the jump turn.

**FIGURE 4-6** Player jumps straight into the air with the arms extended upward.

**FIGURE 4-7** Player turns 180 degrees (in this instance, to the right).

**FIGURE 4-8** Player lands in the ready position.

## SPRINT SKIP

This drill uses the normal principle of the skip, except that on each skip the player tries to jump as high as possible, exploding upward off each leg and using the opposite arm to help drive the body off the ground. This helps to build leg strength and quickness.

## WAVE

The player faces the coach and on a signal turns and runs away from the coach using a drop step first in one direction and then on signal in the other. The player always watches the coach over his or her shoulder and runs in a straight line away from the coach. These skills are used constantly by outfielders catching fly balls and by infielders catching pop-ups.

## BLIND TOSS

The player starts with his or her back to the coach. When the coach yells "ball," the player turns immediately, drops the hips, and looks for the ball. The coach throws the ball up while the player's back is turned and must throw it high enough to give the player plenty of time to turn around and catch the ball. There are many situations in a game when the player may lose sight of the ball and be forced to then find it and catch it.

The player who masters these drills can get a jump on learning softball skills that are directly related to actual play. These lead-up skill drills condition but, more important, teach.

# PREGAME WARM-UP

It is very important to always warm up before each game. This helps to stretch the muscles, get the heart moving, and prepare for the skills that will be used during the game. A typical pregame routine should consist of stretching, running, throwing, and batting.

## STRETCHING

Each athlete works up a personal routine, which should take between 15 to 30 minutes, depending on the athlete. The routine should be consistent and involve all the major muscle groups. Assessment 4-1 illustrates a 30-minute stretch routine for softball.

# RUNNING

Start with some light jogging. The run should last for at least 5 minutes and go for as long as each player needs. Pitchers sometimes like to run greater distances to make sure the body is warm. The player may also structure the run along the foul lines and run between 6 to 10 foul lines. Once the legs feel loose, mark off a distance of 60 feet (the basepath), and run a series of sprints working up to full speed. Jog out to the 60-foot mark and sprint back at three-fourths speed five times in a row; then do it again at full speed.

# THROWING

Partners start about 40 feet apart and slowly stretch out the arm, shoulder, and back muscles with light throwing. After a couple of minutes move back to about 60 feet and increase the hand speed until each athlete is throwing at maximum speed. Infielders finish with snap and quick throws (detailed in Chapter 5), but outfielders finish with long throws working on their crow hop (detailed in Chapter 7).

# BATTING

To prepare for hitting, each hitter starts with a weighted bat of some type and gradually starts building up to a full swing. Some types of hitting warm-ups need to take place either hitting off a pitcher or hitting plastic balls into the fence. Hitters use their normal bats for these drills.

# ADVANCED CONDITIONING AND WEIGHT TRAINING

A program of advanced conditioning and **weight training** can only help the athlete improve his or her performance. The following is a program designed by Diana Neal for the University of New Mexico softball program. This program should only be attempted with a professional trainer. The strength program is conducted twice a week with a weight circuit conducted once a week. The conditioning is performed 3 to 4 days a week. This is only one example of a good weight training and conditioning routine.

Because of the nature of the game, a softball player must stay in touch with his or her body to make sure that muscles don't tighten up, increasing the risk of injury late in the game. Each time at bat the hitter must warm up to some extent to make sure the body is loose. Pitchers must be sure they stay warm even after a long inning when they have been sitting on the bench. Just remember, for the maximum enjoyment and success, always prepare the body physically and mentally and work hard to maintain that level all during the game.

## SUMMARY

- A good stretching program increases flexibility and prevents injuries.
- Conditioning is not just a way to improve skills but also to enhance athletic performance.
- An athlete who has confidence in controlling his or her own body has more confidence in handling other skills. Agility drills, conditioning, and weight training help.

► **Weight Training**

A program of lifting weights to strengthen muscles and help the athlete improve his or her performance.

## Softball Strength Program

### STRENGTH GOALS
1. Emphasize shoulder stability.
2. Improve total body strength.
3. Increase work ethic and mental toughness.

**Workouts**

*Day 1*

| | |
|---|---|
| Jobe shoulder exercises | 1 × 10 (both ways) |
| Step ups | 3 × 10 (each leg) |
| Lunges | 2 × 10 (each leg) |
| Leg curls | 4 × 12 |
| Leg press | 3 × 15 |
| DB (dumb bell) rear delts | 3 × 12 |
| Lat pull downs (behind neck) | 3 × 12 |
| T-bar or machine row | 4 × 12 |
| Low back | 2 × 20 |
| Multi-hip (flexion and adduction) | 2 × 15 (each) |
| Box jumps | 2 × 30 seconds |

*Day 2*

| | |
|---|---|
| Jobe shoulder exercises | 1 × 10 (both ways) |
| Leg extensions | 3 × 10 |
| Lunges | 2 × 10 (each leg) |
| Leg curls | 4 × 12 |
| DB side delts | 3 × 12 |
| DB rear delts | 3 × 12 |
| DB shoulder shrug | 3 × 12 |
| Machine row | 4 × 12 |
| T-bar row | 4 × 12 |
| Bicep curls and tricep press | 3 × 10 ( each) |
| Low back | 2 × 20 |
| Multi-hip (flexion and adduction) | 2 × 15 ( each) |
| Box drills | 2 × 30 seconds |

*Weight room circuit*
Leg extension
Leg curls
Machine row
Pullover
Leg extension
Leg curls
Tricep press
Bicep curls
T-bar rolls

## Softball Strength Program—cont'd

Step ups
Lunges
Air Dyne bike
Footwork drill
Medicine ball torso twist
Plyometric jumps

The athlete does three sets on each machine for 35 seconds with a 10-second rest period. After three sets the athlete moves to the next station. The weight should be set at a medium load with the athlete working as many repetitions as possible in each set.

### Conditioning

The conditioning varies from an oxygen debt run, which consists of endurance mixed with sprints, speed work, stadium stairs, ramps, hills, shuttle test run, and a circuit run.

### GOALS

1. Improve recovery rate, especially for double headers.
2. Increase work capacity, confidence, and a sense of accomplishment.
3. Increase ability to concentrate when fatigued.

### Running Circuit

*Station 1*
One 200-yard run
Athlete has 1½ minutes to run the distance, recover, and be at station 2 ready to go.
*Station 2*
Twelve cone hops
Three sets   set 1 forward
             set 2 lateral-right
             set 3 lateral left
Athlete has 1½ minutes to complete, recover, and be ready for next station.
*Station 3*
Eight 25-yard shuttle runs; done twice with a 2-minute recovery time between each set.
Athlete has 1½ minutes to complete, recover, and move to next station.
*Station 4*
Five repetitions of 5-yard defensive slides (basketball shuffle)
Athlete has 2 minutes to complete, recover, and be ready for next station.
*Station 5*
Four 5-, 10-, 5-, 15-yard sprints
Athlete has 2 minutes to complete, recover, and be ready for next station.

*Continued*

## Conditioning

*Station 6*
Fast feet-sprint 10 yards
Fast feet-back pedal 10 yards
Sprint and back pedals are random and change at a whistle blow.
This drill is for 1 minute with a 1-minute recovery time before the next station.
*Station 7*
Two sets of 10-yard squat jumps (10)
Athlete has a 1-minute recovery before next station.
*Station 8*
15 push-ups
50 crunches
15 birpies with a jump
Athlete is given a 2-minute recovery.

Repeat circuit starting with first station.

## SHUTTLE TEST

### Twelve 25-Yard Shuttle Run

Each athlete runs 25 yards down and back for a total of 12 times. The time is recorded and a 5-minute rest time is started. During this rest time the athlete is encouraged to continue to walk, stretch, and drink fluids.

After a 5-minute rest, the athlete runs the shuttle test again. Time is recorded with both times added and averaged.

### Fast Feet Lateral Up and Back Drill

The athlete moves back and forth laterally across and over boxes for 30 seconds.

### Conditioning

*Oxygen Debt Run*

| Sprint (in seconds) | Jog (in seconds) |
|---|---|
| 45    ←Alternate→ | 45 |
| 45 | 40 |
| 40 | 35 |
| 35 | 30 |
| $O_2$ debt | |
| 30 | 25 |
| 25 | 20 |
| 20 | 60' |
| 20 | 25 |
| 25 | 30 |
| 30 | 35 |
| 35 | 40 |
| 40 | 45 |
| 45 | 2-3 minutes cooldown |

Athletes work on the explosive first step going from jog to sprint.

# Assessment 4-1

Name _____     Section _____     Date _____

## STRETCHING ROUTINE
(total time = 30 minutes)*

30 seconds for each arm

10-20 seconds

10-15 seconds

30 seconds

30 seconds

60 seconds

30 seconds

60 seconds

**9**  Roll back and forth 4 to 6 times

30 seconds

**10**  Roll back and forth crossing legs over 3 times (= 6 rolls)

30 seconds

30 seconds

**12**  Roll out of legs overhead slowly, one vertebra at a time

30 seconds

*From Anderson B, Anderson J: *Stretching,* Bolinas, Calif, 1980, Shelter Publications.

*Continued*

13 30 seconds

14 10-15 seconds

**15** 20-30 seconds to each side

16 25-30 seconds to each side

17 30 seconds

18 15 seconds

19 20 seconds

20 50 seconds

21 60 seconds

**22** Repeat #17, 18, 19, 20, and 21 for other leg

23 10-20 seconds to each side

24 45 seconds

25 Stretch out arms and legs, then relax
5 seconds

Do twice

26 Ab curl

27 Elbow-knee ab curl

28 Alternating
elbow-knee
ab curl

**Stomach workout**
Do each type of ab (abdominal) curl for 20 seconds,
gradually increasing amount of time you do each ab curl to at least 1 minute

**29** Stretch out arms and legs, then relax
5 seconds

Do twice

**30** 50 seconds
Do not overstretch

**31** To right
To left

50 seconds each

**32** 30 seconds

**33** 30 seconds

**34** 30 seconds

**35** Repeat #32, 33, and 34 for other leg

**36** 30 seconds

If using partners, make sure they are far enough apart so they both are getting a good stretch

**37** 15 seconds for each arm

**38** 30 seconds

**39** Ankle exercises should be done every day

# Assessment 4-2

_____ _____ _____
Name                    Section                 Date

## TENNIS BALL EXPLOSION

Two players who act as partners stand about 30 to 40 feet away from the coach. The coach has 10 tennis balls, which he or she throws one after another at or near the players. The players work as a unit calling and catching each thrown ball. As soon as one ball is called or one player moves toward a ball, the coach throws another ball so there is continuous action. With good throws a coach can give the players a wide variety of balls to catch, forcing them to run, dive, and get up and get back into position for the next throw. It's fun and it's great conditioning. Always pay attention to how the balls are being caught, while paying as much attention to fundamentals as to effort.

# Assessment 4-3

Name              Section               Date

## OBSTACLE RACE

In the obstacle course the player must run to an obstacle, jump over it, drop his or her hips to pick up a ball sitting on a base, and throw it (underhand or snap throw) to a teammate positioned at a cone about 90 feet away. They have four obstacles to jump and three throws to make. After the last cone the player then becomes a receiver where he or she moves down the line from cone to cone catching throws from different players before returning to the end of the line. After the receiver catches the thrown ball, he or she then replaces it on the base before moving on to the next receiving position. So the drill moves smoothly, the next player in line does not start the sequence until the player in front is on his or her last throw. Pay special attention to how the player picks up the ball and that he or she makes accurate throws. The receivers must get to their position quickly, get in proper position, and then call for the ball. The entire drill is done at full speed. Discuss errors and what causes them when there is a breakdown in the drill. Run through it about three times.

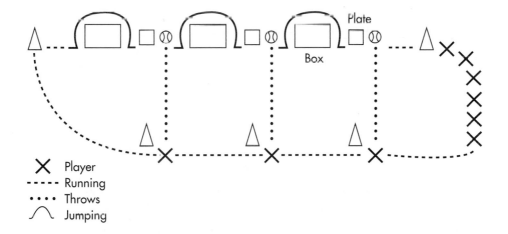

X Player
- - - - Running
• • • • Throws
⌒ Jumping

# Assessment 4-4

Name          Section          Date

## CONE RACE

In the cone race the player runs to a cone and touches the base of the cone with both hands. He or she then runs toward the next cone, jumping over some type of obstacle, and performs the same task over and over. As soon as the first player touches the first cone, the second player takes off in pursuit. Each player must perform the same tasks, but it is a race and the players are trying to catch up to the person in front of them. The coach can place them in order, or he or she can leave the option with first the upper classmen and then the lower classmen. The race promotes competition while demanding certain tasks be performed correctly. If a player does catch the person in front, he or she drops out of the race and gets to take a time off one round. The race can be run in both directions. Usually it takes a couple of times through to get a good workout.

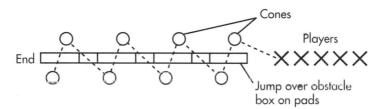

## CONE AND BALL RACE

In the cone and ball race one line of players is running through a series of cones while the line next to them must carry a medicine ball the same distance. Switch lines at the conclusion of each race. One group is working on running a maze, whereas the other must contend with carrying a heavy ball while running at full speed.

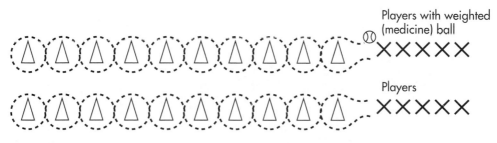

- - - - - Weaving pattern

# Assessment 4-5

Name             Section             Date

## SNAP-THROW RUNDOWN

The snap-throw rundown is a shorter rundown drill where one player starts with a ball and runs full speed at his or her partner. The partner moves toward the player and calls for the ball, sprinting into the catch as he or she would in a game. The player then picks up the partner coming toward him or her and executes the throw. The drill works on snap throws, running, and catching at full speed. As the players tire, bad throws start to show up and more balls are dropped. This is the time when a coach talks to his or her players about concentration and staying focused on the task even when tired. Pay close attention to the proper execution of the snap throw and technique of receiving the throw.

# Assessment 4-6

Name                    Section                    Date

## MULTIPURPOSE INFIELD OR OUTFIELD DRILL

Many coaches schedule multipurpose drills within practice for players to work on certain skills, but we like to incorporate them in conditioning so there are a lot of repetitions at full speed in a short period of time.

For instance, during the first 10 minutes of this drill, the outfielders and coaches are running the infielders through a series of tasks. The third basemen work on retreating to their bags in force situations and for steals; the middle infielders work on turning double plays with and without gloves; the first basemen work on retreating to their bags and receiving bad throws and pickoffs; the catchers work on catching pop-ups and correct throwing position to each bag.

In the second half of this drill, the infielders and outfielders take their positions in the field, and the coaches and catchers run the infielders and outfielders through pop-ups between fielders and fence balls and short fly balls to the outfielders. Not only is the team working on catching fly balls but also on communication.

# Assessment 4-7

Name                    Section                    Date

## PLYOMETRIC MAZE

Coaches use plyometrics in the fall, but it is more fun if a maze or obstacle course is created in conjunction with those box drills and jumping exercises. Use the whole outfield and set up a course. Partner the players and start them at different times to see who can complete the course in the fastest time. Imagination is the only limit, and obviously there are many tasks that can be practiced.

# BASICS OF THROWING AND CATCHING: TECHNIQUE

## OBJECTIVES

*After reading this chapter, you should be able to do the following:*

- Perform the basic throws: overhand throw, snap throw, and underhand toss.
- Describe the mechanics of catching a thrown ball.

## KEY TERMS

*While reading this chapter, you will become familiar with the following terms:*

- ▶ Overhand Throw
- ▶ Snap Throw
- ▶ Underhand Toss

The defensive game of softball can be summed up in two words: throwing and catching. From youth ball to a city league to a national championship, games are won or lost on basic mistakes in throwing and catching. To enjoy the game and be more successful at it, players must concentrate on mastering these basic but important skills.

## OVERHAND THROW

The **overhand throw** is the more difficult, but more common, throw used in the sport. It can produce a much more powerful, faster throw than the underhand toss. To begin, step forward with the right leg so momentum is moving toward the target. Bring the left foot forward while rotating the shoulders and hips and pushing the weight back on the right foot. The left shoulder should be pointing toward the target with the right arm extended back and the wrist cocked.

As the throw is executed, the weight is shifted forward to the front (left) foot. Note that as the throw is made, the arm is brought straight up with a slight bend and with the elbow passing by the head just above the right ear. The shoulders rotate back, square to the target, allowing the right arm to follow through the swing with the hand ending down by the left knee. The back leg then steps through toward the target to complete the overhand throw. See Figures 5-1 through 5-4 to observe this progression. As the ball is released, the wrist snaps down to create the proper 6-12 rotation on the ball and add velocity. The longer the throw is, the higher the release point should be.

# Performance Tip

### 6-12 Rotation

By putting the 6-12 rotation on the ball, the player throws a ball in a direct line to the target. If the throw is made low and hits the ground, it hops directly toward the person making the catch. If the person throwing the ball throws sidearm or comes across the body putting a side spin on the ball, the ball moves off line, depending on the spin put on the ball. If the ball hits the ground in front of the person catching the ball instead of coming right up at that person, a side spin takes the ball off to one side in an unpredictable movement, making the catch much more difficult.

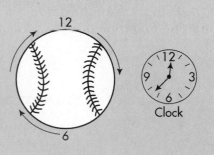

**FIGURE 5-1** Overhand throw. Left shoulder points toward the target. Right arm is extended back and wrist is cocked.

**FIGURE 5-2** Shoulders are square to the target. Right arm passes by the right ear.

▶ **Overhand Throw**

The most basic throw of the game of softball; this is a faster, more powerful throw executed by passing the throwing arm above the ear and following through across the body.

**FIGURE 5-3** Release point.

**FIGURE 5-4** Follow-through by the left knee.

# SNAP THROW

The **snap throw** is used at short distances, during a rundown, for example, to get the ball quickly and accurately to another player without overpowering him or her. It is executed by bringing the ball up to the ear with the arm bent. The arm is then extended, always aiming at the other player's chest. The arm should end up parallel to the ground with the fingers pointing toward your target. Do not bring the arm across the body or follow through past a point parallel to the ground. Bringing the arm across the body causes the throw to be off line, and the extended follow-through increases the chances that the ball will be thrown too low. The snap throw should be practiced every day after the overhand throw. It should be executed with a strong finish to put enough velocity on the ball. Figures 5-5 through 5-7 show the correct progression.

**FIGURE 5-5** Snap throw. With the arm bent, the ball is brought to the ear.

▶ **Snap Throw**

A quick and accurate throw, used to throw short distances. This is performed by holding the ball up to the ear and then extending the arm straight out with the follow-through no farther than perpendicular to the ground and directly toward the target.

**FIGURE 5-6** Arm is extended.

**FIGURE 5-7** Release point. Do not follow through past a point parallel to the ground.

# UNDERHAND TOSS

In many situations, such as a squeeze play at home plate, it may be easier to simply "shovel" the ball to another player with a quick, easy underhand toss without bringing the ball up to the ear. The **underhand toss** follows the same basic principles as the snap throw, except it is an underhand motion. The arm moves in a direction directly at the target. The person tossing the ball needs to stay low, step forward, and stop the forward motion of the arm once the arm is parallel to the ground. Like the snap throw there is no wrist snap. See Figures 5-8 through 5-10 for the correct positions.

**FIGURE 5-8** Underhand toss. Similar to the snap throw but involves an underhand motion.

▶ **Underhand Toss**
    Performed by tossing the ball in an underhand motion (starting from beside the leg) and moving the arm toward the target, stopping at a point parallel to the ground.

**FIGURE 5-9** Move arm directly toward the target. Keep body low.

**FIGURE 5-10** Release point.

## ACCEPTING THROWS

Whenever a defensive player is catching a thrown ball, he or she must do so from an athletic position. Too many players are too casual about catching a ball and do so standing straight up and down with the glove held close to the body. Catching a ball is a skill that should never be taken for granted. The accompanying box provides the basics that must be practiced to ensure catching a ball with consistency.

# Performance Tip

### Catching a Thrown Ball

- Face the person making the throw.
- Drop the hips and keep a slight bend in your legs.
- The feet should be far enough apart to provide proper mobility should the throw be off target.
- Keep the glove in front of the body so to reach out for the ball and bring it into the body with soft hands (giving with the ball to absorb impact).
- If the ball is thrown above the waist, catch it with the fingers of the glove facing up.
- If the ball is thrown below the waist, rotate the glove so the fingers are pointing down. This is the best position for catching the ball.
- When fielding a low throw, lower the entire body, relax the legs, and bend only at the waist.
- Keep the eyes on the ball. Follow the entire path of the ball into the glove. Watching the ball completely into the glove eliminates a number of mistakes.
- Keep the glove open wide. This creates a large pocket for catching the ball. Spreading the fingers within the glove forms an even larger pocket.

## SUMMARY

- In softball the most important defensive skills are throwing and catching.
- The basic throw in softball is the overhand throw.
- The snap throw is used by an infielder in short distance situations when the ball must be thrown quickly and accurately.
- The underhand toss is a quick and easy play used most often in a suicide squeeze.
- Catching a thrown ball is a skill that should never be taken for granted.
- Always work hard on your fundamentals. It will increase your enjoyment of the game and allow you to be more successful.

# Assessment 5-1

Name          Section          Date

## OVERHAND THROW

1. The player steps forward with the left foot bringing back the right arm.
2. The player brings the ball up to a position just over the head.
3. The player throws the ball and follows through past the left knee.
4. Player and partner kneel down with the right knee down and left knee up.
5. With all the weight controlled, the players play catch.

REMEMBER: Focus on reaching back, coming over the top, and accelerating the arm.

## SNAP THROW

With a partner, a player holds the ball in front of his or her face and practices throwing the ball with a stiff wrist. Next, the player brings the ball back to the ear and practices accelerating the arm to a point parallel to the ground. The target area should be the partner's chest. To practice the rundown, one player with the ball can run toward the receiving partner to simulate the rundown.

## CROW HOP

1. Practice a big aggressive hop by jumping over a cone.
2. On landing, there should be a wide base of support with the right arm back and fully extended.
3. The weight should be on the back (right) leg.
4. Initially, the player should throw the ball but not pick up the back foot (thus holding the weight back).
5. Throw in a straight line to the target, not across the body.
6. Eventually the player picks up the back foot with the focus being on the follow-through.
7. Players may finish off the throw with a somersault to emphasize a big follow-through and weight shift forward.

NOTE: The crow hop is further discussed in Chapter 7.

# CHAPTER 6

## PLAYING THE INFIELD: SKILLS

## OBJECTIVES

*After reading this chapter, you should be able to do the following:*

- Have a basic understanding on how to catch a ground ball.
- Know how to approach and catch a pop-up.
- Know the various responsibilities of each infield position.
- Know where the players in general position themselves on the field.

### KEY TERMS

*While reading this chapter, you will become familiar with the following terms:*

- ▶ Drop Step
- ▶ Pick Your Hop
- ▶ Pop-Up
- ▶ Ready Position

While the outfielders are often hoping for more action, the action in the infield is usually nonstop. While there are more strategy games in fastpitch, there is still a high level of intense play even in the slowpitch infield. There are four distinct positions (first base, second base, shortstop, and third base) and each have a multitude of responsibilities. Some of the challenges that face the infielder include the following:

- Catching ground balls, pop-ups, line drives, bunts, and slaps
- Throwing underhand toss to snap throws to overhand throws
- Protecting the bag from stealing opponents (fastpitch only)
- Turning double plays
- Working as relay, cutoff, and tandem players
- Communicating with all players on outs, upcoming plays, and positioning
- Working with the catcher on pickoff plays (fastpitch only)
- Handling rundowns

There are no short cuts to being a good infielder. Every ground ball is different. Every situation is just a little bit different. Players who like making split-second decisions should like playing the infield. Many books have been written on infield skills; it would take an entire book to give an in-depth description of all the skills that must be mastered. This chapter covers the basics that every infield player must know before trying to play a game. Defensive play and positions are discussed further in Chapter 11.

# READY POSITION

Infielders should stand in the **ready position** whenever play is about to commence. The stance should be comfortable, somewhere between standing erect and squatting down, with the feet just about shoulder width apart and your body weight slightly forward. The glove should be open with the pocket of the glove directed toward home plate and in front of the body. Figure 6-1 shows the proper ready position.

**FIGURE 6-1** Ready position.

# Performance Tip

## Pick Your Hop

The first concept an infielder must understand is picking the right hop. This decision is critical since it places the infielder in the correct position to field the ground ball in front of the body. An infielder must learn to pick a spot between where the ball starts and the fielder is standing, at which point the fielder will catch the ball.

# FIELDING

As an infielder, once you **pick your hop** and determine where you will field the ball, you should move into the ball by throwing out the legs farther than shoulder width apart, enabling you to drop the hips and reach out for the ball. The arms are fully extended in front of the body with the back of the glove touching the ground.

The hips should be down, with the back almost to the ground. Soft hands are very important, as the player wants to give with the impact of the ball, bringing it into the body and watching it constantly with the eyes (see Figures 6-2 and 6-3).

If a fielder mishandles a ball, he or she should always pick it up bare handed. Never pick it up with the glove as this wastes valuable time.

▶ **Ready Position**
The stance a player should take in preparation to catch a throw.

▶ **Pick Your Hop**
Picking a spot between where the ball starts and where the fielder stands where the fielder decides to catch the ball.

**FIGURE 6-2** Arms extended, hands out reaching for the ground ball.

**FIGURE 6-3** Give in to the ball, bringing it into the body.

## MOVEMENT

When a ball is hit to an infielder, the infielder should position his or her body in front of the ball. Infielders should always lead with the glove in any direction they move. On balls hit directly at the infielder, the player moves in under control, charging only on the slow roller. The infielder picks his or her hop and then moves in to the ball.

A player should never back up on the ball. If a line drive is hit directly to an infielder, he or she must charge and block the ball, keeping the head down and watching the ball all the way into the glove. Even if the ball is not fielded cleanly, a line drive allows plenty of time to pick up the ball and make the play for the out.

Drop step.

On balls hit away from the infielder, the player must execute a **drop step.** The infielder drop steps at full speed and arcs to align the body in the proper fielding position. This technique is accomplished in three steps: the drop step, the angle, and the arc. (The drop step is discussed further in Chapter 7.)

In the first step, the infielder opens the hips to gain depth. The lead leg determines the proper angle for pursuing the ball, while the opposite leg follows the same path. The fielder uses the angle to gain depth and cover more ground in pursuit of the ball. The third step starts with a deceleration of foot speed at the top of the angle, enabling the fielder to arc into the path of the ball. The top of the angle is one running stride away from the anticipated path of the ball. Until this point, the infielder should be running at full speed. The purpose of the arc is to allow the fielder to position the body in front of the ball so the shoulders can square to the base where the throw needs to be made.

# THROWING

Infielders always throw overhand. This throw is preferred because of the true rotation it puts on the ball and the velocity that it creates. Certain plays from a shorter distance may require a snap throw or an underhand toss instead (as described in Chapter 5).

# POP-UPS

When a **pop-up** is hit, move toward the ball, keeping the arms in a natural running position. Do not move with the glove up in the air.

Catch the ball in front of the body. On all balls hit over the player's head, use a drop step to run back at full speed and get in the best position to catch the ball. Do not drift back slowly and catch the ball over the head.

Pop-up.

▶ **Drop Step**

A technique used by an infielder that allows the fielder to approach a ground or fly ball in the most efficient manner and gain depth on those balls hit away from the fielder or over the fielder's head.

▶ **Pop-Up**

A short fly ball hit in the infield or just beyond the infield.

# FIRST-BASE RESPONSIBILITIES

In slowpitch the first baseman plays deeper and more toward second base, so he or she plays a bigger role in fielding balls. Once a ground ball is hit to another fielder, the player must move quickly to first base to accept the throw and try to make the out. Where the first baseman is positioned depends on the hitter. Figures 6-7 and 6-8 at the end of the chapter demonstrate the potential player positions based on an average hitter and a right-handed power hitter.

In fastpitch the first baseman has greater responsibilities and must be able to play the bunts and slaps just as well as the hard hits. Against average hitters the first baseman stays about 10 feet from first base toward home plate and off the line. With a fast left-handed hitter or slapper at home plate, the first baseman must play much closer to field the ball quickly and throw out a player who can run from home plate to first base in about 2.5 seconds. Playing this position in fastpitch is a constant strategy game that tests the first baseman's ability to read the hitter and adjust to all kinds of hits, slaps, and bunts. Figures 6-9 and 6-10 at the end of the chapter demonstrate infield positions based on an average hitter and a left-handed batter.

## ACCEPTING THROWS AT FIRST

On a ground ball hit to the infield, the first baseman in fastpitch is playing in front of the base, so that he or she must turn toward the infield and retreat to the base. In slowpitch the first baseman plays behind the runner, so he or she must run forward to the base.

With the shoulders square to the throw, the first baseman places both heels on the infield side of first base (facing the person throwing the ball). Slightly crouched with the left foot slightly in front of the right foot and the feet far enough apart to stay mobile, the player looks for the throw.

When the throw is made, the first baseman must decide whether the ball can be caught, whether it can be caught in the air, or whether to stretch out to drop down and block it.

If the ball cannot be caught while staying on the base, the first baseman must leave the bag to make the play. If the ball can be caught in the air, the first baseman waits until the last second, planting the back foot on the infield side of the bag, and then stretches to meet the ball. (*Note:* Right foot is back for right-handed player; left foot is back for left-handed player.) As the back foot is lifted and comes back to the bag, the weight is shifted forward as the player stretches for the ball. The most common fault is to stretch too soon. Figures 6-4 through 6-6 demonstrate first-base stretches.

On balls hit to either side of the base, lunge in the direction of the throw but continue to keep contact with the bag with the back foot. Even on throws wide to the right, keep the back foot on the bag and execute a crossover step to get maximum distance on the stretch.

On balls thrown to the player's left that bring the player off the base, he or she must catch the ball and in the same motion sweep across the line, attempting to make the tag on the runner.

If the throw is made directly at the bag but is too high to catch on the bag, the ready position allows the player to leap up to attempt the catch. If the ball is thrown in the dirt, the first baseman must decide whether to stretch and catch it on the short hop or drop down and block the ball. The important task is to stop the ball.

Left-handed first baseman retreating to base in fastpitch (shows position in front of first base toward home plate).

Left-handed first-base ready position—waiting for the throw (fastpitch and slowpitch).

**FIGURE 6-4** First base—stretch forward with gloved hand extended (left-handed player).

**FIGURE 6-5** First base— stretch left (left-handed player).

**FIGURE 6-6** First base— stretch right (left-handed player).

# PLAYING SECOND BASE

In a slowpitch game the second baseman plays deep in the infield and anywhere from close to first base to behind second base depending on the type of hitter. Since there are no bunting or stealing plays, this player can concentrate on fielding.

In fastpitch the second baseman must also be very mobile but again must try to "read" the batter to determine the type of hitter or bunter at the plate. Because bunting is a major part of the fastpitch game, the second baseman has a lot of responsibilities in covering first base when the corner players move in to field bunts. As a result, where the second baseman plays varies according to his or her own speed, the game situation, and the type of batter. In general, the second baseman plays deep in the infield toward second base where the majority of balls are hit, but if a slap bunt situation (see Chapter 9) is happening, the second baseman must move up to the baseline and be prepared for a hard slap to his or her area or run to first to receive the throw from another infielder. It is a difficult position to play, which requires as much game sense as ability.

# PLAYING SHORTSTOP

In slowpitch or fastpitch, the shortstop usually makes the majority of the plays. Where the shortstop is positioned depends on his or her ability and the hitter. In slowpitch, since there is no stealing or bunting allowed, the shortstop is free to play a great distance from second base and as deep as his or her arm will allow.

In fastpitch covering second and third bases on steals and handling slap bunt offenses is a major part of the game, and it restricts where the shortstop can be positioned. Like the second baseman, the shortstop in general shades the middle, since that is where the majority of balls are hit; but based on the hitter or the baseman at second, the shortstop may also move closer to the third base area or in the baseline halfway between second and third. It all depends on the situation.

# PLAYING THIRD BASE

Fast reflexes are a must for any third baseman because they generally have little time to react to hard hits. In slowpitch the third baseman plays behind the bag and toward the third base line. For a right-handed pull hitter the third baseman may play very deep, even just off the grass. For the left-handed hitter with similar ability, the third baseman could shift over toward the shortstop.

In fastpitch the third baseman has difficult decisions for each batter, since he or she must be ready to play hard hits, as well as drag bunts and slaps. A good third baseman must be able to take away bunts and cannot be afraid to play close to the batter. The strategy game between the hitter or bunter and the third baseman is one of the interesting aspects of the fastpitch game. Figures 6-7 through 6-10 show various situations and proper positioning in fastpitch and slowpitch.

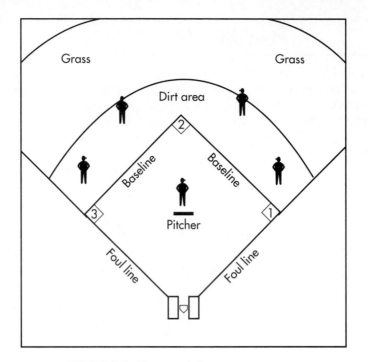

**FIGURE 6-7** Slowpitch basic positioning.

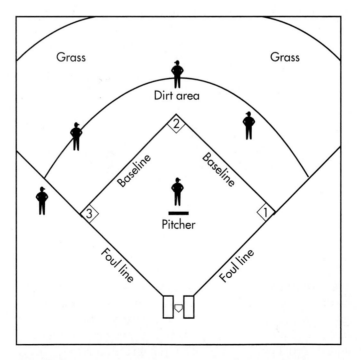

**FIGURE 6-8** Slowpitch shift for power hitter (right-handed).

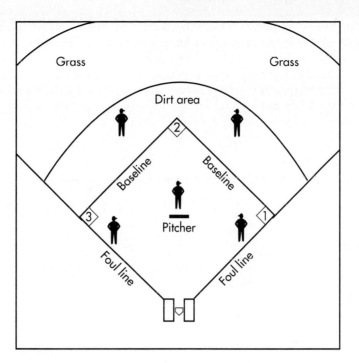

**FIGURE 6-9**  Fastpitch basic positioning.

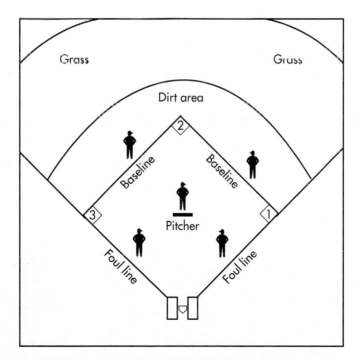

**FIGURE 6-10**  Fastpitch slap bunt defense (left-handed batter).

An infinite number of plays and situations are possible in softball, particularly in fastpitch softball where stealing and bunting add new dimensions to the defensive responsibilities. Infielders must always be aware of outs, where the next play must be made, the speed of the hitter, and any base runners on base. The infielder must be in control at all times and talk on every play. Calling fly balls and instructing other players on positioning or where the next play is anticipated can make the difference between a good play and making an error because of uncertainty.

## SUMMARY

- There are four distinct positions in the infield, each with a variety of responsibilities.
- A good infielder knows how to pick his or her hop and use the drop step on balls hit away from him or her.
- Infielders must be aware of the outs, the next play, the speed of the hitter, each base runner on base, and the score.

# Assessment 6-1

Name          Section          Date

## GROUND BALLS

1. The best progression is to start from a stationary position with the feet farther than shoulder width apart. A partner rolls the ball directly at the fielder, who practices bending down, dropping the hips, and reaching out for the ball. In the first couple of steps of the progression it is best not to wear the glove. Using bare hands forces the fielder to use two hands to catch the ball and teaches the fielder to get down farther and have soft hands. From there the player is allowed to take a couple steps into the ball, and eventually the balls are thrown and hit from normal infield distances.

2. A drill that is good for corner players but can help all infielders is a reaction drill in which an infielder takes 10 ground balls one after the other. The coach hitting the balls hits all types of grounders (ground balls), forcing the infielder to make decisions on when to get down and catch each ball. This is also a good drill for conditioning purposes.

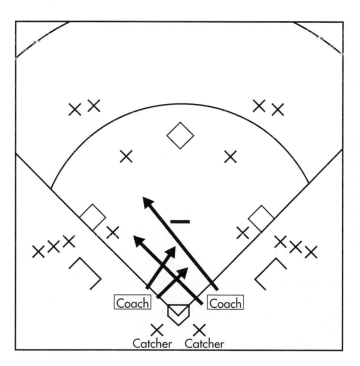

*Infield drill:* Ground balls. One coach hits to right side while other coach hits across to left side. This gives infielders lots of ground balls in a short time.

3. A line of infielders stand along the back side of the dugout (if made of solid material) or a wall. The first player in line throws the ball against the wall that is fielded by the second player. After fielding the ball, the second player then throws it against the wall for the third player and so on. It is a continuous drill that gives the infielders a lot of repetitions. It can be done with or without a glove and with any kind of ball.

Infielders should take at least 10 minutes a day of ground balls. The best way to get the most ground ball practice in this amount of time is to have the infielders take their positions on the field. A coach stands on either side of home plate. Each coach can have someone to catch for him or her or just use one catcher. The coach on the third base side hits ground balls to second and first base players, while the coach on the first base side hits balls to the shortstop and third basemen. Coaches alternate hits so throws won't be coming in at the same time (see illustration on p. 73).

## POP-UPS

1. The easiest way to teach pop-ups is to set a batting machine at home plate and put a set of infielders in their positions. Anyone can feed the machine as it throws high pop-ups. The coach or teacher then walks around making sure infielders are getting back hard and catching the balls in the proper position.

## POSITION PLAY

Multipurpose drills are the best. These involve two coaches or players to run the drills.

1. One coach stands behind the pitcher's mound and rolls balls to the middle infielders as they work on double plays. At the same time a second coach stands at home plate and rolls or hits bunts for the corner players, pitchers, and catchers to field. An extra first baseman takes the throws at first. Middle infielders turn double plays but don't throw to first. (See p. 75, upper illustration.)

2. One infielder is at each position. A line of runners is at second base, and a coach with a bat is at home plate. The catcher, third baseman, and shortstop are working on throwing out the runners attempting to steal third. The pitcher and first and second basemen are working on hits or bunts and throws to first. The drill starts when the pitcher throws to the catcher (either overhand or underhand). The coach either stands there and makes no attempt at the ball (in which case the bag belongs to the third baseman) or shows a bunt (in which case the shortstop must take the bag on the steal because the third baseman must honor the bunt). The catcher throws to the base regardless of which infielder covers it. After the throw crosses home plate, the coach rolls a ball to the first baseman or pitcher, and that player makes the play at first. (See p. 75, lower illustration.)

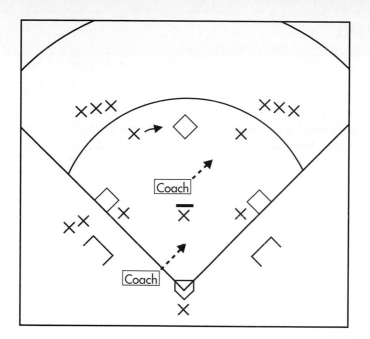

*Infield drill:* Middle infielders working on double plays; corner players, pitchers, and catchers working on throws to first baseman.

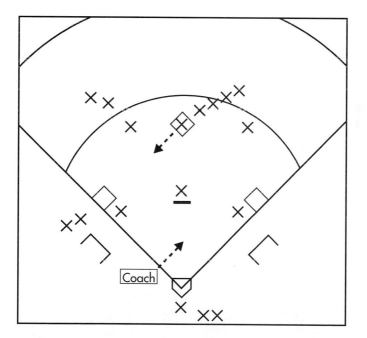

*Infield drill:* Catcher, shortstop, and third baseman working on throwing out runners attempting to steal third. Pitcher and first and second basemen working on handling bunts.

3. One coach at home plate runs a drill for the pitchers, catchers, and corner players while a second coach (off to one side) handles the middle infielders. The
coach stands in the batter's box with a ball. The drill starts when the pitcher pre-
tends to pitch the ball. The coach either throws to the backstop (to simulate a
passed ball), throws a pop-up to anyone, or rolls the ball in front of home plate
(to simulate a squeeze bunt). Meanwhile, the second coach is working on pop-
ups with the middle infielders.

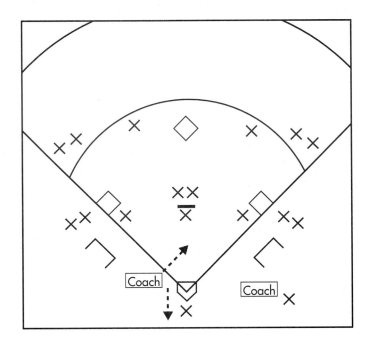

*Infield drill:* Coach at the plate works with catcher, pitchers, and corner players;
second coach works on pop-ups with the middle infielders.

# CHAPTER 7

## PLAYING THE OUTFIELD: SKILLS

## OBJECTIVES

*After reading this chapter, you should be able to do the following:*

- Know the basics of catching a fly ball.
- Describe how to approach various fly balls.
- Know the proper way to handle ground balls.
- Describe the throws that an outfielder must learn.

## KEY TERMS

*While reading this chapter, you will become familiar with the following terms:*

- ► Backup Positioning
- ► Crow Hop
- ► Do-or-Die Play (Situation)
- ► Drifting

One of the most underrated positions in softball is outfield. Playing the outfield is more difficult and complicated than it looks from the bleachers. One of the toughest battles for any outfielder is maintaining concentration, since great periods of time may elapse with no direct action. When action does occur, it comes quickly; for the outfielder who is daydreaming or drifting, it can be embarrassing and sometimes disastrous. In addition to learning fundamentals, a good outfielder also must study his or her backup responsibilities to prevent further damage should an infielder make a mistake. The team defense relies on everyone doing his or her job.

## BASICS: CATCHING THE BALL

The ready position for the outfielder is the knees slightly bent and the feet square facing home plate. The weight is on the balls of the feet, and the glove is held waist high. Outfielders must assume that every hit is coming to them. Never overplay a ball to the right or left, but stand square.

In catching the fly ball, the outfielder wants to gain a position behind the ball, maintaining eye contact all the way into the glove. The hands should stay at the sides of the body until the initial movement up to catch the ball. When catching the ball, both hands should move to just above and in front of the head, with the arms almost fully extended. As the catch is made, the arms absorb the impact of the ball by bringing the glove and the ball to the chest.

Preparing to catch a fly ball.

Catching a fly ball.

## MOVEMENT

One of the most common errors that an outfielder makes is to take a step forward or back the instant the ball is hit. Outfielders should hold their ground until they know exactly where the ball is going and then move quickly to the ball. A step in the wrong direction is much worse than the split second lost while a well-trained outfielder makes the proper decision. When running to the ball, keep the arms in a natural running position, don't stick the glove up early, and run on the balls of the feet to avoid excessive head movement created when running on the heels.

When the ball is hit over the fielder's head, he or she must retreat at full speed, getting to the ball as soon as possible and fielding it in the best position to throw the ball. Think of trying to outrun the ball, instead of just running to the ball. This helps a young outfielder learn to get behind the ball, catching it in front of him or her in

# Performance Tip

## Outfielder's Checklist

Before the ball is hit, the outfielder should know the following:

- Number of outs
- Score
- Speed of the hitter
- Speed of any base runners
- Wind conditions
- Field conditions
- How the pitcher is pitching
- Tempo of the game

All these factors help the outfielder determine where he or she must be positioned, where to throw the ball if it is hit to the outfielder, or where to go for a backup position should the ball be hit to someone else.

Once the ball is hit, the outfielder must do the following:

- Determine where the ball is hit.
- Move at full speed toward the ball, running with the glove down and eyes following the ball.
- Get in the best position possible when catching the ball, converting to the throw as soon as possible (if a throw is necessary).

the best possible position for the subsequent throw. An outfielder should never drift or time a catch. **Drifting** invites errors and increases the chances of base runners advancing to the next base if the fielder is out of position to make the throw. On balls hit to the right or left, be prepared to arc or surround the ball in an attempt to catch it over the throwing shoulder while squaring to the base you may have to throw to. Never run flat across (directly across toward the ball) for a hard hit ball; rather execute a drop step, creating a proper angle on the ball and creating a better chance to catch up to the ball because of the angle. On hard-hit balls that the fielder may or may not catch, all the outfielder can do is run hard and make the best attempt to catch the ball.

# FIELDING GROUND BALLS

There are three different options to deal with ground balls hit to the outfield. On the average ground ball where there is no threat for the ball to get by, the outfielder may just field it like an infielder. On a hard-hit ground ball, the fielder must drop down on one knee and use the other leg, the body, and the glove to block the ball. To control the ball, the fielder must get down before the ball gets too close.

Line up the ball with the center of the body. With a runner in scoring position and a ground ball hit to an outfielder, the outfielder must execute a **do-or-die play**, so named because if the fielder doesn't execute the play, a run will score, which in some cases may be the winning run. To prevent the run from scoring, run hard but under control, leaning over and scooping the ball up with the glove off the side of the left foot. In one motion move right into a crow hop (see p. 82), throwing the weight back and then executing the throw to home plate. Figures 7-1 through 7-3 show the progression of a do-or-die play.

Blocking a hard hit ground ball.

**FIGURE 7-1** Do-or-die play—bending for the ball.

**FIGURE 7-2** Scooping the ball with the glove by the left foot.

**FIGURE 7-3** Picking up the ball in preparation for a crow hop.

▶ **Drifting**

Timing the flight of a flyball with movement of the body so that both will arrive at the same point simultaneously.

▶ **Do-or-Die Play (Situation)**

If a runner is in scoring position and the ball is hit to an outfielder, it is considered a do-or-die situation because if the outfielder does not execute the play correctly, a run will be scored.

# OUTFIELD THROWS

Outfielders always throw the ball overhand. The arm extension creates more velocity and distance. Also, because of the rotation put on the ball, there will be a truer, more direct flight of the ball. When throwing to an infielder, the fielder should always aim at the chest, but any throw chest high to the dirt is acceptable. On long throws make sure it is a line drive and low, since it is the quickest and can be cut off by an infielder if necessary.

The **crow hop** helps the outfielder throw for longer distances by using the body and the arms. Figures 7-4 through 7-6 show the progression of a crow hop. As the

**FIGURE 7-4** After picking up the ground ball, prepare for the crow hop.

**FIGURE 7-5** Step forward with the right leg, moving the weight to the back leg.

**FIGURE 7-6** Lower body is stable with weight at midline point. Arm accelerates forward, followed by weight and step with back leg.

fielder catches the ball, he or she steps forward with the right leg. The fielder then skips on his or her right foot, rotating the left shoulder toward the target, while maintaining weight on the back leg and extending the right arm back. As the throw is executed, the weight is shifted forward to the front foot, the shoulders rotate back square to the target, allowing the arm to come through with the hand ending down by the left knee. The longer the distance, the higher the release point. The initial steps should always be in the direction of the target. The hand moves directly toward the target and not across the body.

# BACKUPS

The correct **backup positioning** for an outfielder in all situations is detailed in Chapter 11. Remember that a fielder should be positioned far enough away from the player he or she is backing up to catch a ball that is overthrown. Stay at least 30 feet away from the player to ensure reaction time and depth to make the catch. Also assume that the ball will be missed and maintain a ready position to make the play.

## SUMMARY

- Playing the outfield is more difficult and complicated than it looks because it demands different skills in both catching fly balls and ground balls.
- With ground balls an outfielder can field like an infielder, blocking the ball with the body or fielding it on the run in do-or-die situations.
- The overhand throw is the basic throw. All outfielders must be proficient at the crow hop because it is the most effective way to make long throws.

▶ **Crow Hop**

A throwing motion that generates maximum velocity on the ball by shifting the weight onto the back leg as the arm is extended back, then shifting the weight forward behind the hand to add power to the throw.

▶ **Backup Positioning**

A fielder moving behind a teammate to be in position to stop the ball in case of an error.

# Assessment 7-1

Name         Section         Date

## WAVE DRILL

The athlete faces a coach with a ball. On signal the athlete starts to run at full speed away from the coach using a drop step. The coach points left and right at different times to force the athlete to turn and run using a drop step with the left foot and then the right foot. At a certain point the coach then throws the ball. This is a footwork drill that also teaches the outfielder to watch the ball all the time.

## SHOULDER TOSS

An outfielder starts facing the coach and then drop steps and runs hard in one direction. The coach then tosses a ball over the proper shoulder. The athlete learns to run hard and stick up the glove at the last second to catch a ball over his or her head.

## CATCHING SHORT FLYS

An outfielder starts about 100 feet from the coach, who either hits or throws a ball at some distance in front of the fielder. The fielder must make the decision on whether the ball can be caught and react accordingly. If the ball can't be caught, the fielder breaks down quickly, drops the hips, and fields the ball like an infielder.

## ARCING

An outfielder starts about 100 feet from the coach, who can either hit or throw fly balls to the player's left or right. The fielder is given a target where the ball needs to be thrown and is practicing arcing the ball (surrounding the ball to catch it over the throwing shoulder and facing the target) so he or she will be in good position to make a quick throw to the base. The balls must be hit or thrown high enough to allow time for the fielder to get around the ball.

## THROWS TO BASES

With the outfielders in positions around the field, the coach hits a variety of balls with the focus on the throw. Infielders are positioned at each bag to receive the throws. On short fly balls, the outfielders must use a quick short throw to the bag. On the throw to home plate, the outfielders must use a crow hop. On balls hit to the fence, the outfielder must run, pick up the ball, and make a strong overhand throw to a relay person.

## GROUND BALLS

By throwing or hitting, all outfielders work on fielding the three different types of ground balls: those fielded easily like an infielder, those that are hard hits and must be blocked, and those ground balls that must be picked up on the run in a do-or-die situation. The fundamentals must be established before attempting these off the bat.

## GAME SITUATIONS

With a pitcher on the mound and two infielders to accept throws, the outfielders are placed at their positions. Hitters at home plate then hit and run the bases with all but infield pop-ups allowed to travel to the outfield. The coach sets up plays so the outfielders can practice game situations.

# CHAPTER 8

# BASICS OF **PITCHING** AND **CATCHING:** TECHNIQUE

## OBJECTIVES

*After reading this chapter, you should be able to do the following:*

- Understand the basics of pitching in both slowpitch and fastpitch.
- Execute fundamentals from the catching, receiving, blocking, and throwing positions.
- Have a better understanding of the responsibilities of pitchers and catchers in softball.

---

### KEY TERMS

*While reading this chapter, you will become familiar with the following terms:*

- ▶ Balance Point
- ▶ Down Position
- ▶ Grip
- ▶ Pitching Rubber
- ▶ Power Point
- ▶ Premotion

- ▶ Shift and Block
- ▶ Slingshot Delivery
- ▶ Up Position
- ▶ Windmill Delivery
- ▶ Wrist Snap

On defense, because the pitcher and catcher handle the ball much more than anyone else, these two positions play a major role in the sport. Pitchers may throw between 80 and 100 pitches to the catcher in any game. The effectiveness of these pitches and how the catcher handles them have a major impact on the team's success or failure. In slowpitch the pitching delivery is less complicated because the rules favor the hitting game. In fastpitch the pitcher may challenge the hitter with both speed and movement, and it may take years to master the skills for success. This chapter details the fundamentals that must be learned to pitch and catch in softball.

# SLOWPITCH DELIVERY

The purpose of the slowpitch motion is not to gain speed or quick movement but to instill control and find the right arc to make it a difficult pitch for the hitter to drive. The pitcher faces the batter with one or both feet on the **pitching rubber.** In a slow half-circle **slingshot delivery,** the ball is brought back behind the body and then forward toward home plate. The pitcher must create an arc that is no less than 6 feet and no more than 12 feet high and is restricted to moderate speed. The weight transfer to the front foot is not explosive but gradual. The ideal pitch has the ball reaching its maximum height at a point close to the batter. The ball then descends as it crosses home plate and will be even with the batter's back shoulder, often causing the hitter to pop the ball up. The slowpitch pitcher may move the ball around the corners of home plate, and it is legal to create any type of spin. A good pitcher changes arm speed and motions to deceive the batter. Grips are a matter of preference, but a backhand delivery, side spin, or dead spin is used to affect the hitter's timing. The slowpitch strike zone is that space over any part of home plate between the batter's back shoulder and front knee.

# FASTPITCH DELIVERY

The slowpitch pitcher is restricted to an arc and moderate speed, but the fastpitch pitcher is in a better position to control the hitter. Pitchers may use the slingshot motion, as in slowpitch, or the **windmill delivery,** which is considered the best because it generates more power. The windmill style is described here, as it is the dominant style. Many have felt that the pitcher dominates the fastpitch game and have tried many ways to decrease the pitcher's control. The pitcher has been moved back, forced to use a new ball, and has even been threatened with a new bat. There are various styles and many philosophies of pitching. Men, because of great upper body strength, tend to throw more with arms and back. Women must be more fundamentally sound and more efficient. Slowpitch is considered the player's sport. Fastpitch spectators are drawn to the amazing skills of the pitcher. As in baseball, many pitches can be learned, and the speed and movement can be incredible.

**FIGURE 8-1** Fastball.

# FINGERS AND GRIP

The ball is held in the fingers. Spins are created as the fingers apply pressure to the seams and the wrist snaps in different ways. The **grip** is firm but not tight. Squeezing the ball too tightly tightens the muscles in the hand, wrist, and forearm. Either a two-fingered grip, which makes the ball float more, or a three-fingered grip can be used. Grips for various pitches are illustrated in Figures 8-1 through 8-5.

**FIGURE 8-2** Rise.

**FIGURE 8-3** Curve.

**FIGURE 8-4** Drop.

**FIGURE 8-5** Change.

► **Pitching Rubber**

A rectangular rubber base that marks the proper pitching distance and can be used for pitching off.

► **Slingshot Delivery** *related to the slowpitch delivery*

A pitching style used in slowpitch where the ball is brought behind the body and then forward toward home plate.

► **Windmill Delivery** *related to the fastpitch delivery*

Pitching style used in fastpitch in which the pitcher makes a circle, starting in front of the body, swinging over the head, and ending just after the hand and arm pass the right hip.

► **Grip**

A specific hold on the ball that generates a certain type of spin on the ball.

# ELEMENTS OF A FASTPITCH (RIGHT HANDER)

## ▶ Wrist Snap

A strong **wrist snap** is crucial in creating speed and movement. The pitcher must cock the wrist on the upward swing and snap it at the **power point** by the hip. This point, which varies for every individual, refers to the point where a perfectly timed snap results in the maximum force on the ball. On the fastball the snap and follow-through point directly at home plate with the first and second fingers the last to leave the ball.

## ▶ Arm

The arm acts like a whip and should be relaxed throughout the pitching motion. A pitcher needs maximum acceleration on the downswing (with complete arm extension for leverage) and should rotate in a smooth plane parallel to the body.

## ▶ Shoulder

No pitch is made with the shoulder. The shoulders move naturally as the hips rotate, following the action of the arm and hand and not leading them. The pitcher never uses the right shoulder to lead the action or create action on the ball. As in hitting, the left shoulder should not spin out prematurely but should open along with the hips to prepare for the arm and then close as a natural finish to the pitch.

## ▶ Hips

The hips act as a coil, storing power to be unleashed just as the hand passes the power point. The hips rotate toward third base to allow the hand a smooth passage by the body. If the hips square too soon, it forces the hand to come around the hips, restricting the ability to snap the ball properly and moving the hand off the proper line.

## ▶ Left Foot

The stride of the left foot should be thought of as a step and not a falling or lunging action. It is a controlled motion and not a fall resulting from a premature weight shift forward. The step should be straight toward home plate with the left foot landing at no more than a 45-degree angle to the plate. The stride is about 4½ steps of the pitcher's own foot. In the delivery the left foot makes contact with the ground just before the ball is snapped.

## ▶ Weight Shift and Balance Point

The weight must be kept back until that explosive moment when the ball is snapped and all the power is thrust forward. The **balance point** varies for each pitcher, but it's like a collection point where the weight remains over the back foot. It occurs just before the pitcher begins the explosive movement down the back side of the arc for home plate. An improper weight shift can create a number of problems, including turning the hips too soon and getting the upper body out of alignment. All these mechanical problems lead to lack of control, speed, and movement.

## ▶ Right Knee

The right knee bends toward third base as the body is moving toward the balance point. This allows the body to push the hips through and opens the shoulders and hips.

## ▶ Premotion

The **premotion** is a natural motion each pitcher uses to prepare for delivery. It is a controlled motion that mentally prepares the pitcher. Personal preference plays a major role in this style.

## ▶ Pitching Rubber

Rules vary in different divisions on whether one or two feet must be on the pitching rubber when starting the delivery.

Pitching.

▶ **Wrist Snap**
A very quick "snap" of the wrist used by a pitcher to create more speed and spin.

▶ **Power Point**
The point at which the wrist snap should occur in a pitch to generate speed; the proper release point occurs somewhere in this power point.

▶ **Balance Point**
For a right-handed pitcher, the point in the pitching delivery in which the right hand is at its highest point above the head and the left foot is at its highest point above ground while maintaining a balanced position on the left foot.

▶ **Premotion**
Natural motion executed by a pitcher to prepare for the delivery.

# PITCHERS AND DEFENSE

The pitcher must be well schooled in defense since he or she can play a major role in that aspect of the game. The slowpitch pitcher may be chosen for his or her skills in fielding balls. That is not the case in fastpitch, but the better fastpitch pitchers are also known for their ability to field their position. Fastpitch pitchers can, however, play a major role in the bunting game by moving quickly to bunts and making the appropriate plays. Also, they will be asked to back up certain bases when a play is anticipated there. Backup responsibilities are discussed further in Chapter 11.

# CATCHER

In fastpitch catching is very demanding, but in slowpitch the catcher has it a bit easier. Although there is still the threat of a collision at the plate, the slowpitch catcher does not have to worry about passed balls, foul tips, steals, or bunt situations. Catchers in both games stand as close to the plate as the hitter allows. Since the ball is on a downward arc in slowpitch, the catcher can assume a comfortable sitting position, placing the glove out and down to catch the ball before it strikes the ground. The fastpitch catcher's life is much more complicated.

When there is no one on base, the catcher assumes the **down position** by squatting behind home plate with the weight on the balls of the feet. The glove hand is extended away from the body, showing the pitcher an open glove and a large target. To further increase the size of the target, the catcher aligns the glove to the center of the body. The free hand is held behind the legs or back to protect it from tipped balls. Figure 8-6 illustrates the correct down position.

Whenever there are runners on base, the catcher must be in the **up position.** This position allows the catcher to shift and execute a throw quickly on a steal. In this position the feet must be at least shoulder width apart with the left foot slightly in front of the right. The back remains parallel to the ground with the hips held high. It is important not to drag the hips. The glove hand should be extended away

Pitcher in ready position for batted ball.

**FIGURE 8-6** Down position.

from the body, providing a large target. Again, the free hand is protected. Figures 8-7 and 8-8 demonstrate the up position.

FIGURE 8-7  Up position (front view).

FIGURE 8-8  Up position (side view).

▶ **Down Position**

The catcher's position in which he or she squats behind home plate with the weight on the balls of the feet.

▶ **Up Position**

The catcher's position when there are runners on base. In this position the hips are higher than in the down position and the back is parallel to the ground, allowing the catcher to shift his or her weight easily if a throw must be made.

# SIGNALS AND TARGETS

In fastpitch every pitcher and catcher must have a series of signals that call between the two players the type and location of each pitch. The catcher gives the signal to the pitcher who may accept it or call it off. The catcher gives the signals with the right hand between his or her legs and the glove placed outside the left knee, covering the area between the leg and the ground to prevent a coach from stealing the signs. Once the signal is given and the pitcher accepts it, the catcher sets into position. When giving a target, the catcher always holds the glove away from the body with the arm slightly bent. The fingers should be spread to make the glove wide open and the glove should stay in the center of the body, not off to one side.

**FIGURE 8-9** Shifting left.

**FIGURE 8-10** Blocking (left).

# SHIFT AND BLOCK (FASTPITCH ONLY)

In fastpitch when a wild pitch is thrown in the dirt with runners on base, the catcher is required to **shift and block** the ball to prevent the runner from stealing a base. There is no need to block the ball when no one is on base, since a passed ball does not result in anyone advancing. Figures 8-9 through 8-12 show the proper positions on shift and blocks. When a ball is thrown in the dirt to the catcher's right, the catcher must step out with the right leg, keeping the pitch in the center of the body. The left leg is then dragged toward the ball while the glove drops down in between the legs to prevent any hole for the ball to sneak through. When the ball is being fielded, the back side of the glove should be on the ground. The same basics apply to a ball thrown to the left side.

**FIGURE 8-11** Shifting right.

**FIGURE 8-12** Blocking (right).

► **Shift and Block**
The movement of the catcher to block the ball if the pitch is thrown into the dirt so no runners can steal a base.

When a pitch is thrown in the dirt in front of the catcher, he or she must smother the ball by jumping out toward the ball and sliding into and surrounding the ball with the legs. The glove again drops down to the ground between the legs to prevent the ball from passing through. The back should be bowed and the chin brought to the chest to protect the throat area and help keep both eyes on the ball. Figure 8-13 illustrates this position.

**FIGURE 8-13** Blocking a ball thrown in the dirt.

# STEALS (FASTPITCH ONLY)

Throwing out base runners is one of the enjoyable aspects of being a fastpitch catcher. When a base runner is stealing second, the catcher leans into the ball just before catching it. As the ball is caught, the catcher executes a jump turn, rotating the shoulders parallel to the batter's box. The glove hand is brought quickly to the ear, meeting the throwing hand. The throw is then executed by transferring weight from the back leg to the front leg, rotating the shoulders and following through hard. The right hand continues down to the left knee, while the back leg follows through to second base. Make sure the initial step is directly at the base to ensure proper alignment. See Figures 8-14 through 8-17.

With a runner attempting to steal third on an inside pitch, the catcher executes a shuffle step behind the right-handed hitter to throw the ball to third. On an outside pitch to the same batter, the catcher steps toward the pitcher, with the right leg moving in front of the batter, clearing a path for the throw. For any pitch to a left-handed batter, the catcher simply steps forward toward third with the left leg and executes the throw as usual.

**FIGURE 8-14** Leaning into the catch.

**FIGURE 8-15** Throw begins. Weight is on the back leg.

**FIGURE 8-16** Weight is transferred to the front leg, following the hand.

**FIGURE 8-17** Follow-through in a direct line to the target.

# FIELDING BUNTS (FASTPITCH ONLY)

In addition to his or her duties behind home plate, the catcher must be ready to take charge of all bunts or topped balls that land just in front of the plate. The catcher must circle around the ball, pointing the left shoulder toward the appropriate base, pick up the ball with a bare hand, and execute the throw. If the bunt is near the first base line and the runner is blocking the throw, the catcher should step back off the line and then throw.

# POP-UPS

Pop-ups around home plate allow the catcher to make a put-out. After the ball comes off the bat, the catcher immediately looks for the ball. As the catcher is turning, he or she removes the mask but does not throw it until the ball is located. Once the ball is located, the catcher throws the mask in the opposite direction, moves to the ball, and catches it over his or her head. On a ball that is popped to the infield side of home plate, the catcher must hustle and get around the ball by turning his or her back to the infield. This puts the catcher in a better position to adjust to the spin on the ball. On pop-ups close to the fence, the catcher should run quickly to the fence and then move away from the fence to make the catch.

# PLAY AT HOME PLATE

The play at home plate (tagging out the incoming runner at the plate) is always exciting. Everyone watching is anticipating whether an out will be made or a run will be scored. It's a play that every catcher lives for, and to be successful he or she must be willing to stand firm and withstand a hard hit.

When receiving a ball for a force out, the catcher moves to the front of the plate and squares his or her shoulders to the ball. The right foot should be on the plate to allow the catcher to stretch the farthest in the same manner as the first baseman (refer to Figures 6-4 through 6-6). On tag plays, the catcher must be prepared to block the plate. After the ball is hit, the player moves to the front of the plate, again squaring up his or her shoulders for the throw. The left foot is placed on the front corner of the plate. No matter where the throw comes from, the catcher must drop the hips lower than the ball to make sure a ball that skips can still be stopped. On a close play the catcher drops the left knee to the ground, blocking the plate with the shin guard. The ball should be held in the glove with the free hand to protect it against impact. If there are fewer than two outs and other runners on base, the catcher must jump up after the play to prevent other runners from advancing.

## SUMMARY

- Although in slowpitch the pitcher is restricted in what he or she can do, in fast-pitch the pitcher can challenge the hitter with both speed and movement.
- Using the preferred windmill delivery, the fastpitch pitcher uses hand speed and various grips to attack the hitter.
- Not only does the catcher receive each pitch, he or she must be able to shift and block wild pitches and (in fastpitch only) throw out base runners.

# Assessment 8-1

| Name | Section | Date |
|------|---------|------|

## PITCHING (FASTPITCH)

### Snap Drill

Have the pitcher stride out with a catcher some 30 feet away. The pitcher practices each pitch using the correct grip and spin. The focus is on the release point and snap.

### Delivery Breakdown

Each pitcher should be forced to break down the delivery from the first step to the balance point to the power point and to the follow-through. Each section isolates a different point in the delivery and forces the pitcher to recognize good and bad points in the pitch.

### Chair Drill

To emphasize keeping the weight back, the pitcher puts the left foot up on either a chair or bucket a 1 to 1½ feet off the ground. This forces the pitcher to hold the weight and not transfer it early to the front foot.

### Stride Stopper

If the pitcher consistently has too long a stride, place a towel or carpet out in front where the pitcher will step on it if he or she overstrides. This mental note helps to keep the stride down. Keep the object there as long as the problem exists.

## DEFENSE

### Combination Drill

With a catcher, the pitchers work on pop-ups, passed balls, and squeeze bunts. The pitcher goes through the pitching motion. A coach either tosses a ball to the backstop to simulate a passed ball, rolls it out to simulate a bunt, or throws it up in the air for a pop-up. The pitchers and catchers react to the situation.

## BACKUP RESPONSIBILITY

In batting practice with the outfielders working on throws, the pitchers work on backing up the correct bases. Each pitcher reacts to each hit and moves to the appropriate base.

# PITCHERS AND CATCHERS

**Infield Throws**

With infielders at each bag, a coach hits bunts and ground balls to the pitchers on the mound and instructs them which base to throw to. The pitchers are working on fielding the balls and making the right throw.

# CATCHER'S DRILLS

**Shift and Block (Fastpitch)**

In practicing the shift and block, the catchers, with full gear on, work in the outfield grass with a softball or mush ball. Once the technique is down, the coach tells them which direction to move and then throws a softball that they must block. The workup goes to a harder ball, and eventually the coach does not tell them where the ball will be thrown. From there, the catchers can work off a pitching machine and then a pitcher.

**Steals (Fastpitch)**

From the up position, the catcher receives the pitch and practices the first step out for a throw to second base. After the step a coach checks the position of the weight and the hand. After many repetitions, the catcher actually throws down to second, working on explosion and follow-through. The same steps apply to each base.

**Pop-ups (Fastpitch, Slowpitch)**

To simulate pop-ups the catchers squat behind home plate with a mask on. The coach hits or tosses up a ball, at which time the catcher must stand up, locate the ball, throw off the mask, and move to catch the ball.

**Blocking Home Plate (Fastpitch, Slowpitch)**

While outfielders are working on throws to home plate, the catchers are working on blocking the plate and accepting throws. The catcher squats behind home plate, moves with the hit, and practices the timing of catching the ball and dropping down to block the plate from the runner.

# CHAPTER 9

# BASICS OF HITTING AND BUNTING: TECHNIQUE

## OBJECTIVES

*After reading this chapter, you should be able to do the following:*

- Develop a basic understanding of hitting.
- Understand the fundamentals of hitting.
- Know the basics of all types of bunting (fastpitch only).

## KEY TERMS

*While reading this chapter, you will become familiar with the following terms:*

- ▶ Drag Bunt
- ▶ Finger Grip
- ▶ Hitting Diagonal
- ▶ Performance Zone
- ▶ Push Bunt

- ▶ Sacrifice Bunt
- ▶ Slap Bunt
- ▶ Stride
- ▶ Sweep Swing

One of the most difficult skills in all athletics is hitting. In slowpitch the key to success is developing a fundamental swing and learning when to swing and make contact with the pitch. In fastpitch the batter must hit a ball that is thrown at him or her from a short distance at speeds of 50 to 90 mph. Although the swing remains the same, when to start the swing varies based on the location of the pitch and its movement. A perfect fundamentally sound swing does not lead to success if that swing is started too early or too late. The knowledge of when to start the swing and where to make contact with the ball takes hours and hours of practice. Hitting is so difficult that being successful one third of the time (.300) is the benchmark for a good hitter.

There are those who think the swings for slowpitch and fastpitch are different, but they are not. All the sections of the chapter except "Bunting" apply to slowpitch and fastpitch hitting. Athletes learning to hit should study the correct fundamentals described in the first half of this chapter. The second half covers bunting, which is not allowed in slowpitch but is a major part of the fastpitch game.

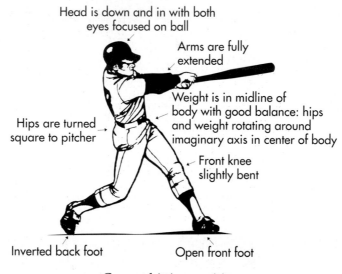

Head is down and in with both eyes focused on ball

Arms are fully extended

Weight is in midline of body with good balance: hips and weight rotating around imaginary axis in center of body

Hips are turned square to pitcher

Front knee slightly bent

Inverted back foot

Open front foot

Correct hitting position.

# FUNDAMENTALS OF HITTING

## ▶ Feet

The back foot should be square to home plate or closed. The front foot should be open at a 45-degree angle or more to allow for a quick transition of the body through the swinging motion. This allows the hips and lower body to move along with the upper body.

Taking a **stride,** the hitter starts with the feet a little more than shoulder width apart. The stride is about 6 to 12 inches past shoulder width and does not include a weight shift to the front foot. The weight stays in the midline of the body.

The step with the front foot should be directly toward the pitcher every time. The key is plate coverage. We do not recommend adjusting the step to the location of the pitch because it is one more movement that can go wrong and mess up the timing. Always keep the step the same. The knees should be slightly bent for a relaxed posture.

Hitting stance.

▶ **Stride**

The step a batter takes with the lead leg toward the pitch as the bat makes contact with the ball.

▶ **Hips**

For a smooth flow of the swing, it is necessary for the hips to follow the bat around the body. Usually this is a natural motion, hindered only by poor positioning of the feet.

▶ **Front Shoulder**

The front shoulder starts slightly down to counter dropping the hands when the swing starts. The shoulder opens naturally with the follow-through and not with the initial action of the hands. When the shoulder is pulled out early, it pulls the hitter off home plate and often results in the hitter pulling his or her head and not seeing the ball all the way to the plate. The hitter always takes a direct line to the ball, bringing maximum force in one direction. When pulling away, a certain amount of that force is lost, moving away from the ball.

▶ **Hands**

The grip that we recommend is the **finger grip,** but even if a traditional grip is used the critical factor lies in proper knuckle alignment and bringing the hands to the ball. Figures 9-1 and 9-2 show proper grips.

▶ **Finger Grip**
A grip in which the bat is held in the fingers, not in the hand, which allows more of the bat handle to be covered, resulting in increased hitting control.

Hip turn.

Front shoulder starts slightly down.

**FIGURE 9-1** Finger grip.

**FIGURE 9-2** Finger grip.

A short compact cut with maximum hand speed is essential for the fastpitch hitter. The bat head follows the hands. Young hitters have trouble understanding hand speed and must work on accelerating the bat.

Inward rotation is also a technique that is often neglected. When a stride is taken, the hands are pushed back in a cocking action. If a hitter strides out, the hands start back. The left arm is not fully extended but just pushed back far enough to create some tension in the front shoulder. The cocking action is back toward the catcher and not around the head.

# Performance Tip

## Finger Grip

A finger grip is one in which the bat is held in the fingers and not in the hand (like a golf grip). The grip covers more of the bat handle, which increases bat control and facilitates top hand hitting. Lay the bat across the fingers of the left hand, angling the handle from the base of the little finger to the tip of the first finger. Then wrap the left hand around the handles, maintaining the angle and creating a V by pointing the thumb and first finger toward the right shoulder. Maintaining these angles, wrap the fingers of the right hand around the bat handle but do not interlock the little fingers. Keep a light grip. The left hand simply holds the bat. The right hand initiates and directs the power.

## PERFORMANCE ZONE

Every hitter must recognize the **performance zone** that contains the perfect spot for hitting every pitch. No matter how hard a hitter works on fundamentals, he or she still must know the critical timing of the swing—*when* to start the swing and *where* to make contact with the ball. The performance zone for each hitter is determined by bat length, arm length, position in the batter's box, and the batter's strike zone. Figure 9-3 illustrates the performance zones for middle, inside, and outside pitches.

## HITTING DIAGONAL

On every swing the hitter wants full arm extension on contact, without dropping the hands as in a golf swing. That means on an inside pitch the ball must be struck way out in front of the plate, while the outside pitch is hit over the plate and off the back leg. In determining the proper contact point for balls that fall between these two extremes, coaches draw a **hitting diagonal** (see Figure 9-3).

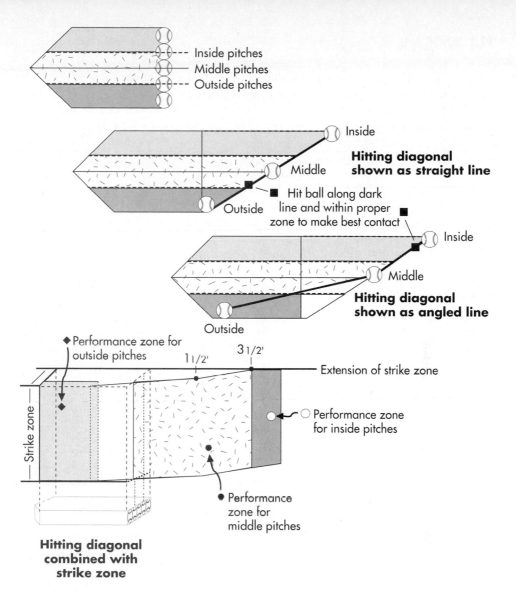

Inside pitches
Middle pitches
Outside pitches

Inside

**Hitting diagonal
shown as straight line**

Middle

■ Hit ball along dark
line and within proper
zone to make best contact

Outside

Inside

Middle

**Hitting diagonal
shown as angled line**

Outside

◆ Performance zone for
outside pitches

1 1/2'    3 1/2'

Extension of strike zone

Strike zone

○ Performance zone
for inside pitches

● Performance
zone for
middle pitches

**Hitting diagonal
combined with
strike zone**

**FIGURE 9-3** Performance zones. At points all along this plane are perfect spots in which to make contact with certain pitches. These points are different for each hitter. The reason why this is so important is because the goal of hitting is TO MAKE PERFECT CONTACT. Hitters need to visualize that all the physical, mental, and emotional skills that come into play are designed for one purpose—to recognize the proper point of contact and figure out how to get the bat there at the same time the ball arrives.

▶ **Performance Zone**

The perfect spot for hitting a pitch. This is different for each batter and depends on the bat length, arm length, the batter's strike zone, the position in the box, and the location of the pole.

▶ **Hitting Diagonal**

A chart drawn to illustrate the proper contact points for inside, middle, or outside pitches.

Since we believe that the outside pitch is hit over the plate, the lines angle down sharply from the pitch that comes over the middle of the plate. Five softballs fit across the width of the plate; therefore when talking about pitch location, the hitting diagonal depicts where the ball travels across the plate.

## INSIDE PITCH

The inside pitch is the pitch the hitter must recognize quickly, since it is the one the hitter must make contact with the farthest from the plate. The pitch that hits the inside part of the plate must be struck some 3 feet in front of the hitter's front foot to have complete arm extension. When the ball is not hit in that area, the hitter must bend the arms or back off the plate in some manner to make contact on the end of the bat.

Arm extension on an inside pitch.

## MIDDLE OF THE PLATE

Middle of the plate is the easiest pitch to hit. The hitter must have the hands about 1½ feet in front of the front foot to have complete arm extension.

# OUTSIDE PITCH

Next to the middle of the plate pitch, the outside pitch is the easiest to hit; however, because hitters don't know how to hit balls in this location or because they lack patience, hitters tend to hit this pitch poorly. In this situation the hitter must wait longer and hit the ball off the back leg while maintaining arm extension.

Where each hitter actually needs to make contact in relation to the plate depends on where that hitter stands in the batter's box. Looking at the performance zone in more depth (see Figure 9-3), the hitting diagonal actually becomes a plane, since the height of the pitch and its affect where it must be struck. The plane is also determined by the hitter's strike zone. This diagonal plane actually creates a hitting zone where a wide variety of pitches pass through, to be hit in a "perfect" spot for maximum performance.

# COMMON ERRORS

The following section examines some of the common mistakes of all hitters. It describes certain problem areas to look for and ways to make changes.

## ▶ Feet

The feet are usually out of alignment because of the hitter's lack of attention to them. When the feet are pointing in the wrong direction, it causes the hips to lock, preventing them from opening toward the pitcher. It also creates pressure on the front knee joint.

Incorrect foot position for hitting.

Correct foot position for hitting.

▶ **Stride**

Many hitters move their left foot away from the plate as they take their stride. See Figure 9-4 for an example of this. This can be caused by a fear element, when the hitter consistently takes a late swing, or if the batter is trying to create more bat speed by torquing the upper body. This results in a **sweep swing.** Recognize when to start the swing and concentrate on taking the step straight at the pitcher.

▶ **Overstriding**

Often the hitter transfers the weight to the front foot too soon, concentrating on throwing the body into the pitch instead of concentrating on hand speed. The stride should be a controlled step, not a rushed lunge. This mistake ruins the rhythm of the swing and leaves the hitter with only the arms to power the bat.

▶ **Front Shoulder Up**

The front shoulder should be slightly lower than the back shoulder. A hitter often drops the back shoulder by using a bat that is too heavy. The higher the front shoulder, the more likely the hitter will develop a hitch or drop the hands in a golf swing.

**FIGURE 9-4** Moving left foot away from the plate.

Overstriding.

## ▶ Sweep Swing

The hands must move directly toward the ball. If the hitter throws the arms out across the back of the plate and then sweeps across toward the pitch it is called sweeping. Again, this may be caused by a heavy bat. In fastpitch batters who sweep are often beaten by good change-ups and hard movement. Some power hitters in slow pitch intentionally sweep and upper cut in an attempt to hit home runs.

Sweep swing.

## ▶ Pulling Left Shoulder Out

Keeping the left side of the body still and the head quiet until after impact gives the hands an opportunity to attack the ball. When a hitter pulls out quickly with the left side, the hitter doesn't see the ball hit the bat and pulling off the plate makes hitting outside pitches difficult. Figure 9-5 demonstrates this problem.

▶ **Sweep Swing**

A common but incorrect swing that occurs when the batter extends the arms straight over the plate and then sweeps across the plate to make contact.

**FIGURE 9-5** Pulling left shoulder out.

▶ **Improper Hand Position**

The hands should be held just above or just below the shoulder. Anything lower than that leads to hitting under the ball and hitting pop-ups. Also check to make sure the hands are off (near) the back shoulder. The hands should never be forward from the midline of the body or closer to the pitcher.

Hands too far below shoulders.

Hands too far away from body.

# BUNTING (FASTPITCH ONLY)

Many types of bunts are used in fastpitch. The **sacrifice bunt** is used to advance a base runner by forcing the defense to make a play on the batter or base runner. The **drag bunt** has the same basic fundamentals but different timing and is attempted for a base hit. A **push bunt** is really a sacrifice bunt that is placed to a particular spot on the field because the corner players are overplaying (rushing in quickly) the bunt. In most cases the bunter is simply trying to push it past a in-rushing first or third baseman to force the pitcher to field the ball and make the play at first (allowing the runner to advance to second or third). The **slap bunt** is executed differently from the right and left sides, but the basic idea is to force the middle infielders to field the ball or better yet hit a soft ground or fly ball that will result in a base hit.

# Performance Tip

## Bunting (Fastpitch Only)

- Stand in the front of the batter's box.
- Pivot on the balls of the feet, shifting 75% of the weight to the front foot.
- Drop the bat angle to 45 degrees.
- Bring the head of the bat forward just in front of the face.
- Bend and relax at the knees.
- Make sure the bat is in front of the plate and covering the entire plate.
- Watch the ball hit the bat.
- Direct the bunt with the bottom hand.
- Hold the bat with a loose grip.

▶ **Sacrifice Bunt**
A simple bunt used for the purpose of advancing a base runner by forcing a play on the batter.

▶ **Drag Bunt**
A bunt that is executed at the last minute for an infielder hit.

▶ **Push Bunt**
A bunt in which the batter tries to "push" the ball to a certain spot on the field past rushing corner players.

▶ **Slap Bunt**
A bunt used to force middle infielders to field the ball. This particular bunt is performed differently for a left-handed and right-handed batter.

## SACRIFICE BUNT

The bunter stands in the front of the batter's box to increase the area of fair territory in which to bunt. Instead of picking the feet up and standing square to the pitcher, the bunter should pivot on the balls of his or her feet, shifting 75% of the weight to the front foot. While the bunter is pivoting, the bat should be brought to a 45-degree angle and held forward just in front of the face. The bat should be covering the whole plate. The head should be almost directly behind the bat. The bunter should hold the bat with the fingers in a loose grip and direct the ball with the bottom hand. Figures 9-6 and 9-7 illustrate the sacrifice bunt.

**FIGURE 9-6** Sacrifice bunt—front view.

**FIGURE 9-7** Sacrifice bunt—side view.

## PUSH BUNT

When the push bunt is executed, everything remains the same as a sacrifice bunt except, instead of giving with the ball for a soft bunt, the bunter pushes the bat into the ball, directing it either at the pitcher or to the spaces between the pitcher and first baseman or pitcher and third baseman. It is a soft push, and the bat angle must be maintained to keep from popping the bunt up in the air.

## DRAG BUNT

From the right side the drag bunt is executed just like the sacrifice bunt, except for the timing and the footwork just as contact is made. In drag bunting the bunter waits until the last possible second to drop from a hitting to a bunting position. In the sacrifice bunt the weight is shifted to the front leg, but in the drag bunt the weight is moved to the front foot by executing a hop step (picking up the back foot and then stepping forward to the front foot). This hop coincides with making contact with the ball, so the bunter is actually starting to run down the first base line while in the process of bunting. The difficulty lies in being able to move the body while still maintaining soft hands on the bat and keeping the proper bat angle.

The same basic skills take place from the left side. However, the left-handed bunter may bunt the ball more in the midline of his or her body or even behind the body as the bunter is already moving away from the plate. This technique takes a lot of skill and lends itself to many errors (like dropping the bat head or not watching the ball), but it is a valuable tool for bunters who possess a lot of running speed.

## SLAP BUNT (RIGHT HANDER)

From the right side the slapper starts with the same basic bunting position as the sacrifice bunt. The slapper shows the bat early to draw the corner players in to open the opportunity to slap the ball by the rushing people.

Drag bunt.

While keeping the weight on the front foot, the slapper brings the hands back to the back shoulder with enough time to slap at the ball and make contact in front of the plate. The slapping motion involves snapping the wrist forward in a chopping motion and stopping on contact. The most important key is control and being able to direct the ball to an area.

## SLAP BUNT (LEFT HANDER)

Assuming a batting position, the left-handed slapper wants to choke up on the bat to increase bat control. The swing is a chopping motion with an inside-out cut. The goal is to hit a grounder in the gap between the third baseman and pitcher, toward the shortstop.

The slapper steps with the lead leg toward the back foot, which initiates motion and establishes the timing with the swing. With a cross step (by the left foot) toward the pitcher, the slapper makes contact with the ball just as the back foot hits the ground. The next step is made with the back leg (right) as the step is made to move down toward first base. The inside-out swing is a chopping motion with a normal follow-through.

# Performance Tip

### Inside-Out Swing

In the normal swing the hands are thrown out and away from the body, toward the ball. In the inside-out swing the hands are pulled in toward the body and then pushed out and away on the finish. Hitters who consistently hit with an inside-out swing hit to the opposite field (right field for a right-handed hitter) because of the angle of the bat when it makes contact with the ball.

Left-handed stance.

Slap bunt—step back with the lead leg.

Slap bunt—crossover step.

Slap bunt—contact with the ball.

Slap bunt—normal
follow-through.

# MENTAL GAME

You won't get much argument from anyone in sports that hitting is one of the most difficult tasks in athletics. Even if a player has worked hard on developing a sound fundamental swing, the next step is even more difficult; the hitter must learn to stay focused and beat the pitcher with the mind, as well as the bat.

What it really comes down to is this: A hitter must be able to block out all sights and sounds and thoughts and tunnel in on a ball as it is delivered by a pitcher. The entire world must be compressed into a narrow vision of the ball as it reaches a

# Performance Tip

## Mental Process for Hitting

1. *In the dugout:* A good hitter studies the pitcher and the umpire. Look for tendencies. A hitter learns as much as he or she can before stepping into the box.

2. *On deck:* The process of tuning out begins. Don't visit with other players. Work on relaxing and practicing good cuts.

3. *Signal:* Once the hitter receives the signal from the coach and steps into the batter's box, all the focus is on the hitting zone. From that point on the concentration is on one pitch at a time. Step into the batter's box quietly and under control, clearing the mind.

4. *The Batter's Box:* This is the hitter's sanctuary. Prepare to attack the next pitch and don't back off until it is determined to be a bad pitch. Be aware of the count, but focus on swinging the bat to meet the ball at a given point in the performance zone.

5. *Ball is released:* The mind takes over the body. The stride is taken, the hands cocked, and the fingers relax around the handle. The mind makes the decision on each pitch and sends a message to attack or stop and wait for the next pitch.

6. *If the decision is made to swing:* The commitment is complete. The mind focuses the body on drawing all the aggression to one point in the universe. If the body has been trained properly, all the energy and power will be directed along the hands to the ball, with no parts of the body hindering the smooth flow of strength and speed.

7. *Once contact has been made:* The task is not finished until the follow-through drives the bat through the ball and around the body.

critical point where it must be struck. Hitting is about developing good habits, and the mental ones are just as much a part of the process as the physical ones. The three major areas covered here are the importance of knowing the hitter's best pitch, in fastpitch playing the count to the hitter's advantage, and how a hitter controls his or her emotions.

## KNOWING THE HITTER'S BEST PITCH

The perfect hitter with the perfect swing who has a good understanding of the performance zone should be able to hit every pitch equally well. But that person simply does not exist. Every hitter has certain pitches that they hit better than others. In fastpitch knowing what pitch a hitter hits best, instead of just going to the plate as a free swinger, can make a big difference in anyone's batting average.

That is why it is so important to be ready for the first pitch and each one thereafter. Once a hitter fails to swing at his or her best pitch or misses it, the advantage goes to the

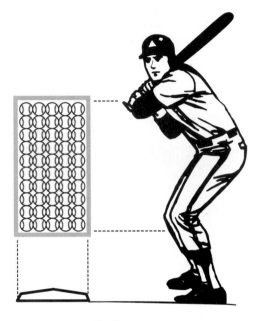

Strike zone.

pitcher, and the hitter may never see that pitch again. When a hitter realizes what pitches he or she hits best (inside or outside, high or low), the hitter learns to lay off other pitches and hit only those he or she can hit well. This brings us to the hitting game played between the fastpitch pitcher and the hitter.

## PLAYING THE COUNT (FASTPITCH ONLY)

Although in slowpitch there is little variety on pitches and the count really does not matter that much, it can make or break the fastpitch hitter. When a batter is ahead of the count (has more balls than strikes), he or she is in control and can be more selective about the pitches. When a batter falls behind, that control is lost, and the hitter must look more to hit strikes. For instance on a 2-0 count, a hitter should never pop-up a rise ball or ground out on a tough curve that breaks hard away from the plate. Those are pitcher's pitches; when given the option, a good hitter wants to lay off those pitches. Here is where the intelligent hitter uses the fundamentals and the mind to beat a pitcher and where a talented hitter with no knowledge of the mental game may not be as successful. Some hitters get into a habit of swinging at bad pitches in practice or being anxious when a pitcher has lost control. Learning these principles can make everyone a better hitter. Remember what is practiced will always show up in games.

## EMOTION

A hitter in any league must have controlled aggression to be successful. Emotion is a very important part of athletics, but it must always be kept under control. A good competitor wants his or her emotion to work as a positive force and not a factor that distracts the hitter from concentration or judgment. In fastpitch a hitter must study the strike zone and play the count, but the primary focus of the slow-pitch hitter is to be patient. Because of the slow movement of the ball, it is easy for a slow pitch hitter to pull out too early, overswing, or take the head off the ball while trying to hit it as hard as he or she can. Good slowpitch hitters don't necessarily try to hit a pitch as hard as they can, but rather try to place the ball to weak areas of the defense. In both games the mental approach to the game is just as important as the physical game.

## SUMMARY

- Hitting is one of the most difficult skills in all athletics.
- A perfect fundamentally sound swing does not guarantee success if that swing is started too early or too late.
- Every fastpitch hitter must also be able to sacrifice bunt. The better players also master one of the other bunts to diversify their game.

# Assessment 9-1

_____     _____     _____
Name                          Section                        Date

## ANGLE BUNTING PROGRESSION

1. Stand in the front of the right-hand batter's box, with a wide stance, the left foot just in front of the right foot. Assume a batting stance with bat in hand and practice going from the hitting to the bunting stance. Concentrate on correct pivot, weight shift to front leg, and correct bat angle and position.
2. Without a bat, stand in the batter's box and have someone toss a softball over the plate and practice catching the ball with the right hand only just at the position the bunter should make contact with the pitch. Start slowly and work up to full speed.
3. Once the mechanics become natural, use a bat and work up from hitting off someone tossing the ball to bunting off a pitcher. Once the foundation is laid, the last step is all timing.

## SLAP PROGRESSION

1. Have the player stand in the left-hand batter's box with a glove on the left hand. Instead of hitting, the player just catches the ball with the glove. The concentration is on the footwork, taking the first step back and then the crossover step forward. The catch should be made just as the second step is made.
2. Working on the inside-out swing, a slapper stands facing a fence. The slapper puts the knob of the bat on the hip and is close enough to the fence for the end of the bat to touch it. The slapper then combines the footwork with the inside-out swing, and the fence forces the slapper to bring the hands in or contact the fence.
3. From here the player slaps off a batting tee working on technique. When the fundamentals are down, then the slapper is ready to work off a pitcher.

# Assessment 9-2

Name                    Section                    Date

## BATTING TEES

Batting tees are great tools for teaching fundamentals. Make sure the tee is set up in front of the plate and not on it. By putting balls in different positions on the tee, a hitter can practice hitting all kinds of pitches.

## GRANADA

The Granada pitching machine will shoot plastic balls at the hitter from a very short distance of 18 feet. Softball size or baseball size can be used. The two primary purposes of this machine are to teach hand speed and contact. This machine is not recommended for those without a fundamental swing, since the quickness will force them to fall into bad habits just to make contact. On the other hand, the softball machine when used at a greater distance is good for young hitters because it is slow and the ball is large.

# Assessment 9-3

Name                    Section                    Date

One way to improve concentration is to hit small balls (golf ball size whiffle balls) with a slender bat. This forces the hitter to concentrate more because both the ball and the hitting surface are very small.

## BATTING MACHINES

Batting machines of all types are great for teaching the fundamental swing because a hitter can get hundreds of repetitions. There are all kinds of machines. Based on how the machine is set and where the hitter stands, all kinds of pitches can be hit. One of the most effective ways to use machines is to set two machines over the same home plate: one throwing inside pitches and one throwing outside pitches. By alternating from one machine to another, a hitter learns very quickly the different timing that is required for inside and outside pitches.

## BALL TOSS

Tossing up a ball and having the hitter drive it either against the fence or into a open field is another good drill that provides a lot of repetitions. Two things to remember, though: first, each swing should be taken at full speed and never rushed; second, the angle at which the tosser throws the ball should always be 45 degrees, so the ball is coming at the hitter and can be hit in front of the plate. Some coaches or other hitters toss the ball from the side, so the hitter is actually hitting the ball over the plate.

## HITTING OFF PITCHERS

Hitting off a pitcher is a must once the hitter has a good sound fundamental swing. A hitter must learn to hit a variety of pitches with all kinds of movement and all kinds of speed. Each pitch is different, and it takes hours of hitting to learn how to hit every pitch. An underhand pitcher is preferred, but anyone who can pitch or throw should be used just to give the hitter the maximum number of cuts.

# CHAPTER 10

## BASICS OF SPRINTING, BASE RUNNING, AND SLIDING: TECHNIQUE

## OBJECTIVES

*After reading this chapter, you should be able to do the following:*

- Know the fundamentals of running.
- Have a broad understanding of the importance of base running in softball.
- Know some rules that make runners attack the defense.
- Understand the best method of leadoffs.
- Know the two basic slides.

## KEY TERMS

*While reading this chapter, you will become familiar with the following terms:*

- ► Base Running
- ► Bent-Leg Slide
- ► Controlled Lead
- ► Head-First Slide

- ► Pickoff Attempt
- ► Running (One-Way) Lead
- ► Sprinting

Every aspect of the game requires good running skills, from base running to defensive movement toward the ball. Every player can learn to improve running skills and become a better all-around player. For many people running is just a natural skill, but for some it requires work. Women especially have been neglected in the area of running skills. Poor running skills obviously affect base running and sliding, so start with the basics and take it one step at a time to be the most complete softball player possible.

# SPRINTING

One of the most essential skills in softball is **sprinting.** Everyone is born with different running skills and natural speed. A softball player is not a track athlete and in many cases is not built like one, but that doesn't mean that a player can't be an efficient runner. The starting point for improvement may be to observe track runners or invite a track coach to class to demonstrate proper running. Watching is always one of the best ways of learning. Next, every runner must learn about explosion and how to run at full speed. Assessments 10-1 through 10-3 list drills to teach these skills. Poor mechanics, lack of knowledge, and lack of emotion often result in a mediocre effort.

## Becoming a Better Runner

1. Try to run relaxed without tightening or raising the shoulders. Don't clench the fists, run with a still neck, or hold the head back.
2. Move the hands and arms back and forth in a plane by the body and hips, not across the body. A crossing movement with the arms throws the momentum and weight off line. The hands should move by the hips, driving the elbows way back and then coming forward. Some people run with short choppy arm movements, which hurts drive and rhythm.
3. Track coaches talk about "bringing the heel to the butt" as a way of describing how to bring the feet up off the ground. A runner must be light on his or her feet, running on the balls of the feet as if running on eggs or hot coals. There should be a rapid movement of the feet on and off the surface.
4. The rhythm of the body working together is a key to running. If the arms are slow and move across the body, the runner's speed is affected. The arms should move quickly and in conjunction with the legs. As the right arm goes up, the left leg comes up and vice versa.

► **Sprinting**
   Running short distances (as from one base to another) as quickly as possible.

# BASE RUNNING

A hitter becomes a base runner the moment he or she hits the ball. **Base running** is one of the most exciting and fun aspects of softball, and yet many runners are able to achieve much better results than they do. A good base runner is a smart runner who challenges the defense and always tries to take the extra base. Always run at full speed and stay alert. The following tips describe some general rules on how to attack the defense.

- On all ground balls, the hitter (turned base runner) runs down the baseline at full speed and does not slow down until after reaching first base.
- When beating out an infield hit, never lunge in the final step into the bag. Hit the bag like a sprinter crossing the finish line.
- After hitting a line drive or a fly ball, always assume there will be an opportunity to take an extra base and make a sharp turn at first base looking for the opportunity to advance to second.
- When a sudden stop is needed, always slide.
- When in a sacrifice situation at first base, always slide into second. Look in when first leaving the base to make sure it is a safe bunt; when approaching second, glance at third to see if someone is covering third base. If no play is being made at second, a smart runner may be able to take an extra base by continuing to third. (Fastpitch only)
- When at second base, look for the opportunity to steal third base. If the shortstop is standing too close to second or the third baseman is not alert, there may be an easy opportunity to take third. (Fastpitch only)
- When scoring from second base, cut third base at full speed until told by the coach to stop.
- Notice where outfielders are positioned when on base so that when a hit occurs, a quick decision based on where the defense is playing can be made. Indecision usually results in an out. Never hesitate and then go.
- When at third base, assume there will be an error. Never be caught by surprise.
- With two outs, take off on contact. Whether it appears to be an easy out or not, run at full speed and continue to run hard until told by the coach to stop. Never assume an out. Always assume an error.

▶ **Base Running**

Sprinting from one base to the next, making your way around the base circuit to home plate.

# Performance Tip

## Every Smart Base Runner Should Know

- Number of outs
- Inning
- Score
- Defensive alignment
- Strength of the outfielder's arm
- Strength of the catcher's arm
- Where the ball is at all times
- Any pickoff plays
- Speed of the base runner ahead of you
- Who is accepting the ball at each bag

## LEADOFF (FASTPITCH ONLY)

The most common leadoff technique is a **running (one-way) lead,** but the most efficient method is a **controlled lead.** The running lead gives a strong catcher the opportunity to pick off the runner, since all the runner's weight and momentum are leaning away from the bag. The controlled lead allows the runner to get the maximum leadoff distance from the bag while still maintaining body control. On concluding the leadoff, the runner lands in a position to move in either direction at a moment's notice, depending on where the ball is hit or if a **pickoff attempt** is made. Figures 10-1 through 10-4 give a step by step illustration of the controlled lead.

The runner assumes a relaxed stance by the bag, with the feet no more than shoulder width apart. The left foot is placed against the side of the bag. Keeping both feet at the same level increases stability and makes it easier for the runner to push off the dirt and bag.

To initiate movement, the runner starts with a short step with the right foot approximately 1½ feet in a direct line toward the next base. Keeping the shoulders square to the infield, the runner uses a crossover step with the left leg and a hard swinging action with the arms to propel the body the maximum distance. At the conclusion of the leadoff, the runner should come down with the feet farther than shoulder width apart and the knees slightly bent and in a stable position.

# Performance Tip

## General Rules for Base Running

- Always take leads in the baseline. (Fastpitch)
- The shortest distance between two points is a straight line.
- With two outs and a full count on the batter, take off with the pitch. (Fastpitch)
- When at first with a left-handed power hitter at home plate, shorten the lead and expect a line drive. Avoid a quick double play. (Fastpitch)
- When at first base with a ball hit to the second baseman, don't run into the tag and give the defense an easy double play.
- When on base with less than two outs, make sure the ball is on the ground or hit safely before taking off. A runner must be aggressive but not reckless.
- When there are runners at second and third and less than two outs, the runner at third should try to score on an infield hit.

▶ **Running (One-Way) Lead**

A very common leadoff technique in which the runner faces the next base and runs toward it. Not as efficient as the controlled lead.

▶ **Controlled Lead**

A leadoff technique in which the runner stays facing home plate and does a cross-over step, landing in a wide stance, which allows easy movement in either direction.

▶ **Pickoff Attempt**

An attempt by the catcher to force an out on a base runner with a big lead.

**FIGURE 10-1** One-way lead.

**FIGURE 10-2** Controlled lead: ready stance—left foot on the bag.

**FIGURE 10-3** Crossover with the left foot.

**FIGURE 10-4** Stable position—ready to move in either direction.

# SLIDING

It is inevitable that every player must slide into base at some point. It is important to learn the proper way to slide to prevent injury. If any player has any doubts at all about sliding, he or she should not attempt it until the skills have been learned. If a runner starts a slide, the player should never try to stop in the middle. As explained in the drills, these skills can be practiced on wet grass or on a piece of wet plastic. This chapter describes just two basic slides.

## HEAD-FIRST SLIDE

The **head-first slide** is the fastest and most dangerous slide, but in many ways is the easiest to learn. As the runner approaches the bag, he or she drops the head and shoulders and pushes off with one leg. The runner tries to land on the stomach, abdomen, and thighs. The hands and arms should be fully extended toward the bag. Sliders must bend at the knees to prevent dragging the feet. The head must be pushed back to prevent the chin from coming in contact with the ground. The hands should be up and reaching for the bag and not under the body. The real danger is not in the slide; it comes from being cleated in the head and hands from the defensive player.

## BENT-LEG SLIDE

The **bent-leg slide** begins 10 to 15 feet from the bag. The slider must drop the hips and shoot out the right leg toward the bag, bending the opposite leg under the knee to form somewhat of an upside down *4*. Glide over the top of the ground, sliding into the bag with the extended heel moving across the top of the bag and the shin of the bent leg hitting up against the bag. When on the ground stay as flat as possible, tucking the chin to avoid hitting the head on the ground when first landing.

Remember that in any slide the runner must have the confidence to run at full speed and slide across the ground. The typical mistake is to slow down, jump up, not out, creating a painful landing.

▶ **Head-First Slide**
One of the two basic slides, performed by diving on the stomach, head first toward the base.

▶ **Bent-Leg Slide**
One of the two basic slides, performed by sliding on the back, with the right foot out toward the bag and the left leg bent behind. Less dangerous than the head-first slide.

## SUMMARY

- Any player can learn to improve running skills to become a better all-around player.
- A smart base runner can make the difference between winning and losing by taking advantage of defensive mistakes.
- To be an effective base runner, every player should master both the head-first and bent-leg slide.

# Assessment 10-1

Name                    Section                    Date

## HEAD-FIRST SLIDE

On a soft, slick surface, the player starts off learning the head-first slide from a standing position. By dropping down over his or her heels, the player learns to shoot out across the surface, landing on the stomach with the head up and arms and hands out. Once the player's confidence is built, he or she starts from a slow run and again on a soft surface drops down and then takes off (jumps off) one leg and throws the hands out trying to land on the stomach. When the runner seems to have a good idea on how to slide, it should be done at full speed. A strip of wet plastic, wet grass, or a sand pit can be used for teaching sliding.

## BENT-LEG SLIDE

For the bent-leg slide, a player drops down on one hand and then, supporting the body with that hand, throws the legs outward, landing first on the buttocks and eventually on the back. Once the player understands how to throw the legs outward, the player should try this from a slow run into a sand pit. When ready, the slide should be done at full speed to force the body to fly out across the surface of the pit instead of dropping down on it.

# Assessment 10-2

Name                               Section                               Date

## QUICK STEPS

Start with the feet, teaching the runners to run on the balls of their feet with quick steps, running as if on eggs. Focus on picking up the knees and bringing the heels to the buttocks area as rapidly as possible. Start with running in place at a slow pace and work up to full speed.

## ARM MOVEMENT

To work on arm movement, the runner sits on the grass with the legs straight out in front. By taking aggressive strong swinging motions, the runner tries to bounce the body off the ground. From here, the runner stands and again uses long swinging movements with the hands, making sure to come straight by the hips and not across the body.

# Assessment 10-3

Name          Section          Date

## CIRCUITS

Practice running a circuit (a single, a double, a triple, a home run). Work on running at full speed, hitting the inside of the bags with the left foot and arcing.

## REACTION DRILL

With a hitter at the plate and a coach throwing the pitches, react to various plays: hit and run, bunt and run, and so on.

## RUN-TAG DRILL

With a coach at the plate and runners at second and third, runners work on reacting to the hit. The runners at second must hold their ground on ground balls hit in front of them or run to third on ground balls hit behind them. Runners at third attempt to score on ground balls and must get back and tag on fly balls.

## HIT-AND-RUN DRILL

With a pitching machine on the field, hitters practice the hit and run. The hitter hits each pitch and then runs out the hit according to where it was hit (single, double, etc). The coach gives directions if there is any question.

# CHAPTER 11

# TEAM DEFENSE: STRATEGY

## OBJECTIVES

*After reading this chapter, you should be able to do the following:*

- Know the correct positioning and fundamentals to handle relays.
- Know where defensive players must position themselves as cutoffs.
- Understand the basics of a one-throw rundown.
- Have an idea of how to turn a traditional double play with a runner at first.
- Understand the importance of the mental game when playing defense.

## KEY TERMS

*While reading this chapter, you will become familiar with the following terms:*

- ▶ Cutoffs
- ▶ Double Play
- ▶ Knee Turn
- ▶ One-Throw Rundown
- ▶ Relays
- ▶ Tandems
- ▶ Trailing Runners

A team is based on each player knowing his or her responsibility. There are some differences between fastpitch and slowpitch based on the rules, but many of the duties are the same. Figures 11-1 and 11-2 show the basic areas of the field that each player controls.

Responsibilities overlap between players, so a dominant player in each area must be designated. For instance, the center fielder is the boss of the outfield, and the outfielder always has the final say between infielders and outfielders. In addition to individual skills, each player must understand the team concept and individual responsibilities. These should be practiced before any games are played. The assessment at the the end of this chapter shows changes in responsibilities based on the offensive situation. In the infield the basic difference between the two games is that fastpitch allows bunting and base stealing, so the infielders must play tighter to counteract these plays. In slowpitch those skills never come into play, so the corner players and middle infielders play much deeper. Both fastpitch and slowpitch outfielders must not only catch fly balls but also back up plays by the infield. In either type of softball outfielders are the last line of defense and must not let a hit or thrown ball get by.

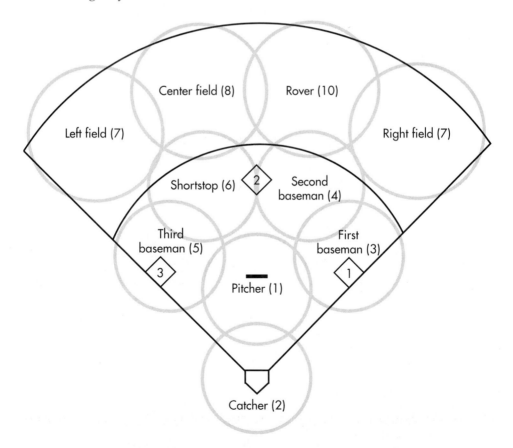

**FIGURE 11-1** Player position in slowpitch softball.

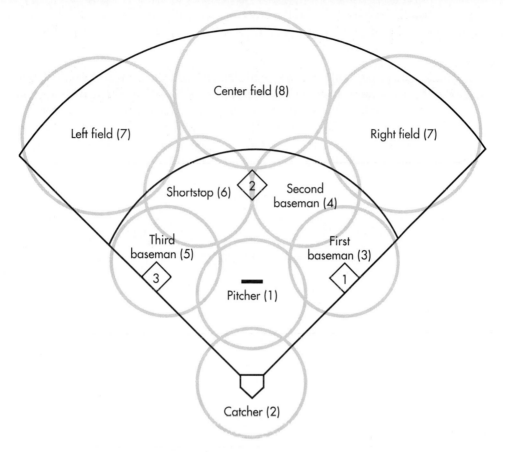

**FIGURE 11-2** Player position in fastpitch softball.

## RELAYS AND TANDEMS

The middle infielders are involved in most **relays.** The shortstop handles all relays from the left and center fielders. The second baseman handles all relays from the right fielder. These infielders must position themselves between the outfielder and the base he or she is throwing to. They must also know the strength of the outfielder's arm to take up a position at the proper distance.

Being able to make a smooth transition from the catch to the throw is the key to a successful relay. In making the play the infielder squares the shoulders to the out-

▶ **Relays**
Returning the ball from the outfield to the infield by using two throws rather than one.

fielder as the relay person catches the ball. In one continuous motion the hips are opened, the left shoulder turns toward the target, and the quick overhand throw is made. The throw must be made from a wide stable base to allow for mobility and power.

**Tandems** are a safety valve when a sure extra base hit occurs. On balls hit to right field, the shortstop leaves the bag and moves to a position between the second baseman and the intended target. The tandem is off the second baseman's shoulder and close enough to catch the ball on the fly should an overthrow be made. The second baseman plays the same role on the other side. The tandem must remember to stay out of the way should a good relay throw be made.

# CUTOFFS

Some teams allow the pitcher to act as a cutoff person, but most teams ask the pitcher to move off the mound and back up the throws at either third or home plate. The first and third baseman work as **cutoffs** and divide the field up according to each coach's philosophy. Some coaches prefer to have the first baseman act as the only cutoff, but some give the third baseman all cuts when the ball is hit to the middle of left field or farther left. The first baseman makes all other cutoffs. The slowpitch pitcher is standing deeper, is often a good fielder, and most often takes the cuts.

Again, the cutoff stands square to the outfielder or infielder making the throw and lines up with home plate. The catcher is also responsible for yelling out commands to help line up the cutoff. To make a large target, the cutoff always holds up his or her arms, keeping the feet spread apart and dropping the hips, so the fielder can move to adjust to the throw. In all cases the cut person assumes the cut will have to be made and backs off at the last minute if there appears to be a play at home plate. Cutoffs must also be aware of **trailing runners** to know what base to throw to should the ball need to be cut. On weak throws to the plate or those thrown off line, a good cutoff can move to the ball and make a quick relay to the player and still assist in the out.

# ONE-THROW RUNDOWN

The **one-throw rundown** evolved from the need for a quicker and more efficient way to handle the rundown. The first rule is that the defensive player (the one with the ball) must run at the base runner at full speed, holding the ball in clear view by his or her ear. The first option is to literally run down and tag the base runner. If the player is unable to catch the runner, the second option involves the throw. As the first defensive player runs at the base runner, a second fielder positions himself or herself inside the baseline and just in front of the base. As the runner is chased toward this fielder, this second infielder accelerates toward the runner and yells "now" when he or she is ready for the ball.

The infielder calls for the ball when the runner is just a few feet from this defender. If the base runner has been forced to run at full speed and the timing is correct between the two defenders, the second defensive player should be able to make a quick tag as the runner attempts to stop or change directions.

## DOUBLE PLAY

One of the most exciting plays in softball and a big offensive strength is the **double play,** when two outs can be made off one play. Double plays occur in a variety of ways and can involve any of the bases. An infielder can catch a line drive and then step on the bag to double-up a runner who was not able to get back in time. A pitcher may throw the ball home for a force-out when bases are loaded, and the

# Performance Tip

### Rundown Basic Rules

- The first option is to run down the base runner.
- The base runner must be forced to retreat at full speed, so he or she is unable to change directions once the ball has been thrown to the second defender.
- A snap throw must be used because it is quicker, more accurate, and reduces the chances of an overthrow.
- The second defender must accelerate toward the base runner as he or she calls for the ball so that the runner will not have time to stop and change directions before the tag is made.

▶ **Tandems**
Middle infielders who serve as a "safety valve" if the throw goes past the intended relay person.

▶ **Cutoffs**
The players (first and third basemen and in some cases, the pitcher) who intercept a throw from an outfielder or another infielder when no play can be made or when another play is foreseen.

▶ **Trailing Runners**
Runners who are trailing the lead base runner.

▶ **One-Throw Rundown**
A defensive play in which the infielder makes a quick out by running at a base runner at full speed and executing a snap throw to a second infielder.

▶ **Double Play**
A defensive maneuver resulting in two outs in one play.

catcher turns and throws to first for the second out. The double play discussed here is the traditional one turned at second base with a runner at first, so the middle infielders are the ones making the play at the bag.

# TYPICAL DOUBLE-PLAY SITUATION

To understand the traditional double play, it is important to understand that if a ball is hit toward right field, the second baseman will move toward first base to back up this position. The shortstop, in turn, will move toward second base.

*From the First Baseman.*   If the ball is hit to the first baseman, he or she either fields the ball with the bare hand or sweeps it into the throwing hand with the glove. When throwing the ball to second base, the first baseman executes a jump turn (illustrated on p. 26) to align the body and attempts to throw to the shortstop as he or she is crossing second base.

*From the Second Baseman.*   There are three basic throws used by the second baseman. When the ball is caught close to second base, the second baseman should execute an underhand toss, allowing the shortstop to simply pick the ball out of the air as the shortstop passes the bag. On balls hit farther toward right field, the second baseman executes a **knee turn.** After fielding the ball, the second baseman rotates the hips toward second base while dropping down on the left knee. The weight is over the hips and the shoulders are square to second base. At the same time the body is getting into position, the ball is taken out of the glove and a snap throw brings the ball to the shortstop. Finally, for balls hit closer to first base, the fielder executes a jump turn, since he or she will need to throw a longer distance. After fielding the ball the defender jumps and rotates the hips 180 degrees, ending up with the left shoulder pointing toward second base. From that ready position a strong overhand throw is made.

*From the Shortstop.*   If the ball is hit to left field, the shortstop or third baseman will relay the ball to second base. The first two throws that can be made from the shortstop are the same as from the second baseman, but the direction obviously would be opposite. On balls hit deep in the hole by third base, the fielder must time the catch to plant the right foot, field the ball, and throw in almost one continuous motion.

*From Third Baseman.*   Because of the angle of the throw, there are no special steps or body positions for the third baseman's throws.

*Accepting Throws at Second.*   There are four basic rules to remember when accepting a throw for a double play. (1)The fielder should run to the bag at full speed, (2) square the shoulders to face the throw, (3) reach out for the ball with both hands, and (4) catch the ball in the pocket of the glove, not the webbing.

On balls hit to the shortstop that carry the shortstop close to second but not close enough to make the play, the second baseman takes the throw off the back of the bag (side farthest from shortstop and closest to right field). With his or her feet shoulder width apart, the second baseman places the left foot on the bag and keeps the right foot about 2 feet behind it. After catching the toss from the shortstop, the second baseman picks up the left foot, rocks back on the right foot, and squares the shoulders to make the throw to first.

# Performance Tip

## Accepting Throws at Second

The fielder should do the following:
- Run to the bag at full speed.
- Square the shoulders to face the throw.
- Reach out for the ball with both hands.
- Catch the ball in the heel, not the webbing.

On balls hit away from second base, the second baseman comes to the shortstop side of the bag at second base and places the heel against the bag. As the second baseman reaches for the ball, he or she picks the left foot up and steps away from the baseline and toward the pitcher. As the catch is made, the second baseman shuffles off the bag into a throwing position toward first base. The same basics apply to the shortstop when he or she receives throws. The assessment at the end of this chapter details different play situations (hits, runners on base, etc.) and the defensive change in positions that should occur.

## MENTAL GAME

Knowledge of the game builds confidence and should not stop with fundamentals. A good player understands the game and the strategy involved. A good player studies the opponent and the situation at hand to anticipate what may be required. Whether an athlete is highly skilled or not, an athlete can increase his or her effectiveness by knowing his or her strengths and weaknesses and getting a jump on the action.

Team defense is all about understanding the game and communication. One of the best ways to prevent mental lapses is to talk to other players about current situations. While on the field players must talk about upcoming hitters and where they plan to position themselves. Players need to communicate to each other on

▶ **Knee Turn**
A turn executed by fielding the ball and turning toward the target as the player drops down on the left knee. This is a method to stabilize the body to execute a good snap throw.

where base runners are and where the next play should go. Remembering a hitter's tendencies (pulling the ball or consistently hitting late, bunting skills, type of swing) also gives the defensive players opportunity to be in the right place at the right time to make the out. Outfielders, who tend to see the least amount of action, should be constantly talking about hitters and upcoming plays.

The dugout is a place to physically rest, but every good player knows this is not a time for a mental time-out. While on the sidelines, players can discuss all kinds of ways to attack the defense. If there are any questions on defensive situations, time in the dugout can be used to iron out any confusion. In softball, players must learn how to relax but must also keep the mind and communication active to prevent errors caused by players who have lost their focus and concentration.

## SUMMARY

- Team defense is based on each player knowing his or her responsibilities.
- In addition to basic plays, middle infielders must know how to handle relays and tandems.
- The corner players, and in some cases the pitcher, must work on acting as cutoffs for throws between the outfielders and the plate.
- The one-throw rundown evolved from the need for a quicker and more efficient way to handle rundowns.
- One of the most exciting and rally breaking plays in softball is the double play when two outs result from one play.
- Softball players must learn to play relaxed and yet maintain focus and constant communication with other players to prevent typical errors caused by players who lose their concentration.

# Assessment 11-1

Name                              Section                              Date

### Single to left field

**No one on base**

- P: Moves to position halfway between mound and 2nd
- C: Follows runner down to 1st
- 1B: Makes sure runner tags base when making turn, then covers 1st
- 2B: Covers 2nd to take throw from LF
- SS: Moves toward LF, making sure ball doesn't get by LF
- 3B: Protects 3rd

**Outfielders**

- CF: Backs up LF
- RF: Moves in toward 1st base area to back up throw to 2nd

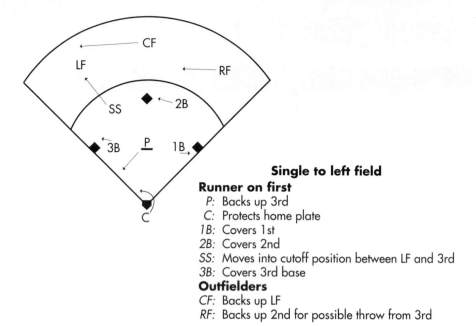

**Single to left field**
**Runner on first**
 P: Backs up 3rd
 C: Protects home plate
 1B: Covers 1st
 2B: Covers 2nd
 SS: Moves into cutoff position between LF and 3rd
 3B: Covers 3rd base
**Outfielders**
 CF: Backs up LF
 RF: Backs up 2nd for possible throw from 3rd

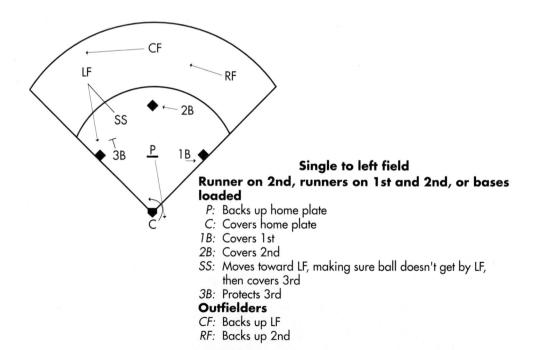

**Single to left field**
**Runner on 2nd, runners on 1st and 2nd, or bases loaded**
 P: Backs up home plate
 C: Covers home plate
 1B: Covers 1st
 2B: Covers 2nd
 SS: Moves toward LF, making sure ball doesn't get by LF, then covers 3rd
 3B: Protects 3rd
**Outfielders**
 CF: Backs up LF
 RF: Backs up 2nd

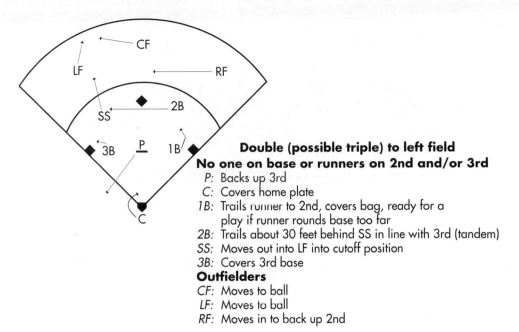

### Double (possible triple) to left field
### No one on base or runners on 2nd and/or 3rd

*P:* Backs up 3rd
*C:* Covers home plate
*1B:* Trails runner to 2nd, covers bag, ready for a play if runner rounds base too far
*2B:* Trails about 30 feet behind SS in line with 3rd (tandem)
*SS:* Moves out into LF into cutoff position
*3B:* Covers 3rd base

**Outfielders**

*CF:* Moves to ball
*LF:* Moves to ball
*RF:* Moves in to back up 2nd

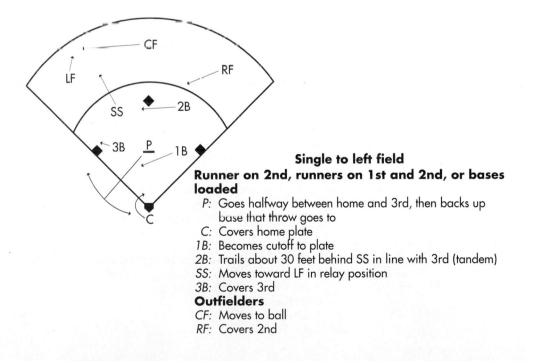

### Single to left field
### Runner on 2nd, runners on 1st and 2nd, or bases loaded

*P:* Goes halfway between home and 3rd, then backs up base that throw goes to
*C:* Covers home plate
*1B:* Becomes cutoff to plate
*2B:* Trails about 30 feet behind SS in line with 3rd (tandem)
*SS:* Moves toward LF in relay position
*3B:* Covers 3rd

**Outfielders**

*CF:* Moves to ball
*RF:* Covers 2nd

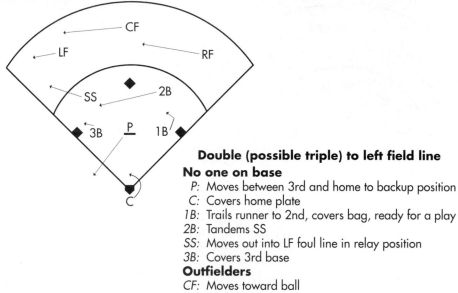

### Double (possible triple) to left field line
**No one on base**
- P: Moves between 3rd and home to backup position
- C: Covers home plate
- 1B: Trails runner to 2nd, covers bag, ready for a play
- 2B: Tandems SS
- SS: Moves out into LF foul line in relay position
- 3B: Covers 3rd base

**Outfielders**
- CF: Moves toward ball
- RF: Backs up 2nd

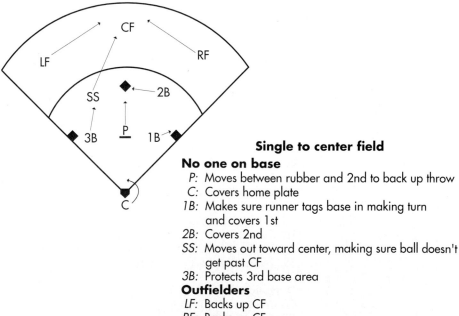

### Single to center field
**No one on base**
- P: Moves between rubber and 2nd to back up throw
- C: Covers home plate
- 1B: Makes sure runner tags base in making turn and covers 1st
- 2B: Covers 2nd
- SS: Moves out toward center, making sure ball doesn't get past CF
- 3B: Protects 3rd base area

**Outfielders**
- LF: Backs up CF
- RF: Backs up CF

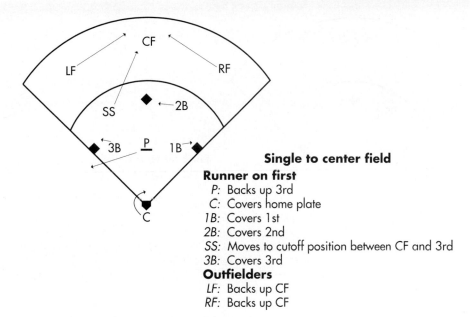

### Single to center field
**Runner on first**
- *P:* Backs up 3rd
- *C:* Covers home plate
- *1B:* Covers 1st
- *2B:* Covers 2nd
- *SS:* Moves to cutoff position between CF and 3rd
- *3B:* Covers 3rd

**Outfielders**
- *LF:* Backs up CF
- *RF:* Backs up CF

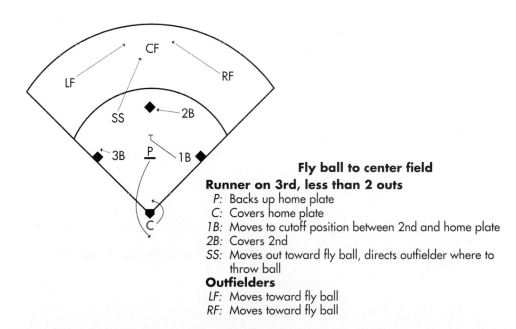

### Fly ball to center field
**Runner on 3rd, less than 2 outs**
- *P:* Backs up home plate
- *C:* Covers home plate
- *1B:* Moves to cutoff position between 2nd and home plate
- *2B:* Covers 2nd
- *SS:* Moves out toward fly ball, directs outfielder where to throw ball

**Outfielders**
- *LF:* Moves toward fly ball
- *RF:* Moves toward fly ball

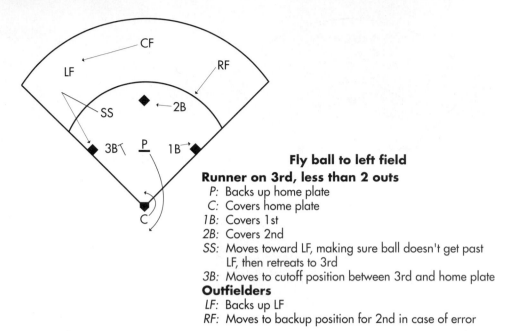

### Fly ball to left field
### Runner on 3rd, less than 2 outs
   *P:* Backs up home plate
   *C:* Covers home plate
   *1B:* Covers 1st
   *2B:* Covers 2nd
   *SS:* Moves toward LF, making sure ball doesn't get past LF, then retreats to 3rd
   *3B:* Moves to cutoff position between 3rd and home plate
### Outfielders
   *LF:* Backs up LF
   *RF:* Moves to backup position for 2nd in case of error

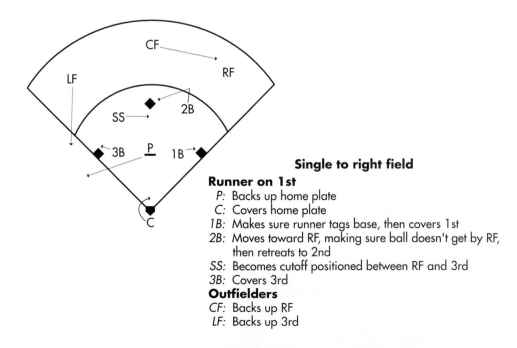

### Single to right field
### Runner on 1st
   *P:* Backs up home plate
   *C:* Covers home plate
   *1B:* Makes sure runner tags base, then covers 1st
   *2B:* Moves toward RF, making sure ball doesn't get by RF, then retreats to 2nd
   *SS:* Becomes cutoff positioned between RF and 3rd
   *3B:* Covers 3rd
### Outfielders
   *CF:* Backs up RF
   *LF:* Backs up 3rd

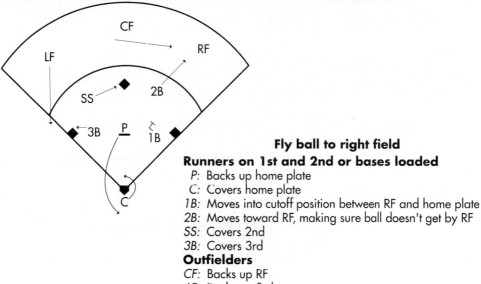

### Fly ball to right field
### Runners on 1st and 2nd or bases loaded
*P:* Backs up home plate
*C:* Covers home plate
*1B:* Moves into cutoff position between RF and home plate
*2B:* Moves toward RF, making sure ball doesn't get by RF
*SS:* Covers 2nd
*3B:* Covers 3rd
### Outfielders
*CF:* Backs up RF
*LF:* Backs up 3rd

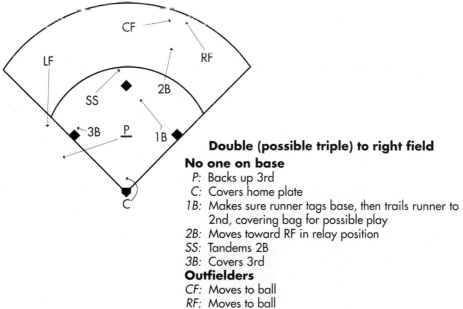

### Double (possible triple) to right field
### No one on base
*P:* Backs up 3rd
*C:* Covers home plate
*1B:* Makes sure runner tags base, then trails runner to 2nd, covering bag for possible play
*2B:* Moves toward RF in relay position
*SS:* Tandems 2B
*3B:* Covers 3rd
### Outfielders
*CF:* Moves to ball
*RF:* Moves to ball
*LF:* Backs up 3rd

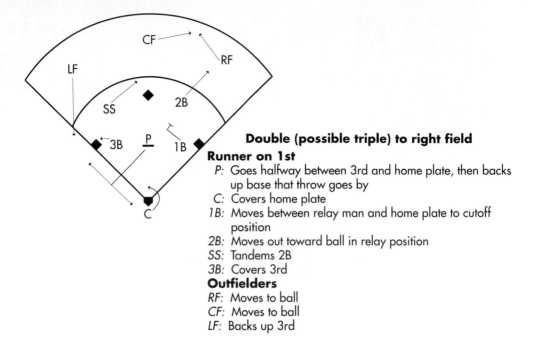

### Double (possible triple) to right field
### Runner on 1st
P: Goes halfway between 3rd and home plate, then backs up base that throw goes by
C: Covers home plate
1B: Moves between relay man and home plate to cutoff position
2B: Moves out toward ball in relay position
SS: Tandems 2B
3B: Covers 3rd
### Outfielders
RF: Moves to ball
CF: Moves to ball
LF: Backs up 3rd

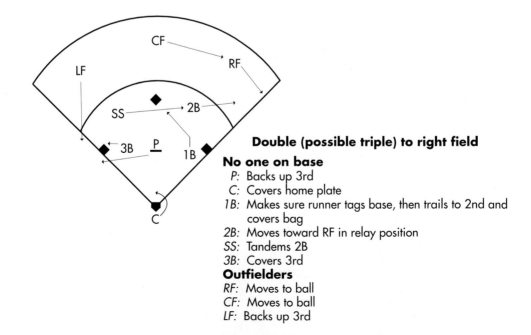

### Double (possible triple) to right field
### No one on base
P: Backs up 3rd
C: Covers home plate
1B: Makes sure runner tags base, then trails to 2nd and covers bag
2B: Moves toward RF in relay position
SS: Tandems 2B
3B: Covers 3rd
### Outfielders
RF: Moves to ball
CF: Moves to ball
LF: Backs up 3rd

# CHAPTER 12

# TEAM OFFENSE: STRATEGY

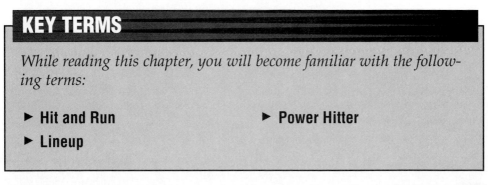

## OBJECTIVES

*After reading this chapter, you should be able to do the following:*

- Understand what goes into making up a batting lineup.
- Know the factors that help a coach determine how best to attack a defense.
- Understand how to use the hit and run play to encourage aggressive hitting and to attack a defense.

### KEY TERMS

*While reading this chapter, you will become familiar with the following terms:*

► **Hit and Run**          ► **Power Hitter**
► **Lineup**

This chapter covers the complex areas of lineups and strategies to give the player insights into the game and help him or her better understand what factors are considered by coaches in making decisions. Softball is a game for all kinds of personalities, and that is especially evident in the fastpitch offensive **lineup.** One of the aspects that makes softball such a true team sport is that each player must define his or her own role on the team—the **power hitter,** the bunter, the runner—no one role is more important than the other for each must do his or her job if the team is to be successful. A three-, four-, or five-slot hitter is much different than a leadoff hitter in skills and in personality. Each player works hard to find their best place on the team, and it is the coach's quest to put together the very best lineup that brings out the best skills in each of the players.

Understanding what is expected of each position in the lineup also helps young players understand why coaches set the lineups as they do. Following are some basics that help determine a team's lineup.

## DETERMINING THE LINEUP

In general, a coach evaluates the team speed and each individual's speed. From practice and scrimmages the coach determines players who hit for power and those that hit more singles but may have a high batting average. Bunting ability is a skill all players must have, but some show the speed and skills to also bunt for base hits through drag bunts or slapping. The accompanying box can be used as a guide for what skills each position in the lineup demands.

# Performance Tip

### Selecting Players for the Lineup

#1: Speed; great batting average; knows the strike zone; good base runner.

#2: Speed; good bunter; knows the strike zone; good bat control.

#3: Best hitter on the team; hits for high average; good RBI hitter; usually a power hitter.

#4: Power; good RBI person; good batting average.

#5: Same as fourth batter but not as consistent.

#6: Either good speed and contact like the second hitter or good RBI but low batting average.

#7-9: Most inconsistent hitters; if possible, look for clutch hitters or good bunters; if you have a batter with a high batting average but few RBIs the eighth position is ideal.

Not every team is made up of players that fit this formula. Some teams have more speed than power. Some teams have more skill than others, but these are the general guidelines. The fun starts now because a coach must decide how best to use the talents on the team. There are many offensive plays in fastpitch, but slowpitch is more of a hitting game. In fastpitch the team can perform all kinds of bunting and stealing plays depending on the offensive talent and the strength of the defense. Although the offense in slowpitch may work more on placing the ball, the offense in fastpitch is diverse and more challenging.

# STRATEGY (FASTPITCH ONLY)

The question of when to bunt and when to steal comes up all the time. Here are some factors that coaches much consider when setting an offensive strategy in fastpitch.

*Speed of the Base Runner.*   The faster the runner, the higher the percentage of success in steals. With slower runners, coaches use more sacrifice bunts, drag bunts, and even bunt and run plays.

*Defensive Alignment.*   If the defense is playing tight at the corners, the coach takes away sacrifice bunts, leaving slaps, steals, and hit-and-run options.

*Strength of Catcher's Arm.*   When a hitter is facing a fast pitcher or a catcher with a strong arm or quick release, it is much more difficult to steal and much better to try some form of bunting.

*Infield Awareness.*   From pitch to pitch a defense changes and so does their discipline. Coaches and players should check to see how the defense is reacting to determine if there is a breakdown in covering bases.

*Number of Outs.*   The number of outs is important because it determines whether the coach has one or two chances to score a run after moving a runner to second base. If there is a good bunter at the plate, followed by a good hitter, the bunt can help; but if the situation is reversed, a coach doesn't want to lose the better hitter just to advance the runner. If there are two outs and a runner at first, it is often best to steal to give the hitter the opportunity to knock in a run.

One of the most exciting plays in fastpitch is the **hit and run.** The runner on base begins to run for the next base right when the ball leaves the pitcher's hand, and the batter is asked to hit the next pitch, unless it is way out of the zone. When using the hit and run, the coach must consider several points.

▶ **Lineup**
The order of players to bat for the offense. This order is very important to the strategy of the offense because each position in the lineup has specific strengths.

▶ **Power Hitter**
As the name suggests, a hitter who hits the ball consistently far, which in turn results in more runs batted in (RBIs).

▶ **Hit and Run**
An offensive play in which the batter hits and the base runner steals on the pitch.

*Speed of the Base Runner.* This comes into play with both a fast and a slow runner. With speed, the play enables the runner to steal, possibly advancing two bases, and avoid the double play. It also allows the hitter to concentrate on just hitting the ball. Also, with the shortstop leaving his or her position to cover the steal, it may open a hole for the hitter. With a slow runner on base, it keeps the team out of a double-play situation and usually guarantees a runner in scoring position.

*Defensive Alignment.* Many times a hit and run is a good call in typical bunting situations. It catches the corners up tight and may force an error. Because of the positioning of the corners it may open up more opportunities for the hitter and provide a better chance to steal.

*Type of Hitter at the Plate.* The hitter must have good bat control and make consistent contact. A big swinger who strikes out a lot is not a good candidate for a hit and run. Contact by the hitter is the most important factor in the hit and run.

*Number of Outs.* The hit and run can be used at any time, but there is always the danger of a double play if the hitter hits a line drive to an infielder.

*Mental Game.* Sometimes when a hitter becomes tentative, takes too many strikes, or is in a batting slump, the hit and run can help to boost the hitter's game. This play frees the hitter from all decisions except to locate the ball and hit it hard. This freedom sometimes helps a hitter. There are some hitters, however, who panic when asked to execute this play and either miss the ball or slow down their bat to make sure they make contact. A coach must evaluate each player to determine who will respond best to this command.

Although slowpitch is pretty much a stand-and-hit game, the fastpitch teams can get very much involved in this exciting strategy game. The smart player or coach can take advantage of another team by trying all kinds of tricks. Be creative. The worse thing an offense can be is predictable.

## SUMMARY

- The formula for the offensive lineup depends on the talent available and the responsibilities of each slot from getting on base to knocking in runs.
- A coach weighs many factors, such as the defensive alignment and the skills of the hitter and base runners in deciding the offensive strategy.
- The hit-and-run play can be a useful tool to attack a defense if the right batter and base runner are in that situation and the pitcher is predictable.

APPENDIX

# GAME PERFORMANCE EVALUATION

Too many times players' evaluation of their game performance focuses on batting average, errors, or winning and losing. The following evaluation was devised to help players have a realistic point system to assess their contribution to the team. Plays that may go overlooked in the statistics may in fact be big plays in helping the success of the team. The best players on any team may not have the highest batting average, but they will always lead the team in positive points.

## HOW POINTS ARE AWARDED FOR PLAYERS

### Positive Points

| | |
|---|---|
| Getting on base (except through a fielder's choice with an out involved) | 5 |
| Successful sacrifice | 5 |
| Score a run (unless a result of being on base through a fielder's choice with an out involved | 10 |
| RBI | 10 |
| Advance a runner with no outs (other than a sacrifice) | 5 |
| Fine defensive play (catcher throwing runner out; great catch) | 5 |
| Fine defensive play (physical or mental) that saves a run | 10 |
| Alert, heads-up baserunning (coach's discretion) | 5 |
| Stolen base | 5 |
| Successful hit and run | 5 |
| Picking up signs or pitches | 10 |
| Pinch hit | 5 |
| Pinch-hit RBI | 10 |

From Craig SB, Johnson K: *The softball handbook,* Champaign, Ill, 1985, Human Kinetics Publishers.

## Negative Points

| | |
|---|---:|
| Physical error that results in a run (including passed balls) | 5 |
| Each additional run that results from an error | 10 |
| Mental error that results in a run | 10 |
| Each additional run that results from an error | 15 |
| Taking a called third strike with runners in a scoring position | 5 |
| Failure to advance a baserunner via a sacrifice | 10 |
| Baserunning error (overrunning a base; not running full speed; not sliding when the situation calls for it) | 5 |
| Poor physical effort | 10 |
| Poor sportsmanship | 5 |
| Being thrown out of a game | 10 |
| Mental error (missing signs; improper backups; getting picked off when a big lead is not needed; lack of communication between defensive players; missing cutoff) | 5 |

# HOW POINTS ARE AWARDED FOR PITCHERS

## Positive Points

| | |
|---|---:|
| Win a game | 25 |
| Save a game | 10 |
| Groundouts (11 or more in a seven-inning game) | 5 |
| No-hitter | 10 |
| One-hitter or two-hitter | 5 |
| Throw 91 pitches in a seven-inning game | 5 |
| Two earned runs or less in a complete game (with shutout, add 5) | 5 |
| Give up two or less walks in a seven-inning game | 5 |
| Issue more than two walks but strikeout ratio is at least 2-1 | 5 |
| Complete game | 5 |

*Relief Pitchers*

| | |
|---|---:|
| Come in with runners on base and do not allow a run to score, except through error | 10 |
| Face tying or winning run without allowing it to score during the late (fifth to seventh) innings | 15 |
| Outstanding relief job (coach's discretion) | 5-10 |

## Negative Points

| | |
|---|---:|
| Walk that later results in a run | 5 |
| Additional walk that results in a run that same inning | 10 |
| Walk that forces in a run | 10 |
| Walk after being ahead 0-2 | 10 |
| Giving up a hit on 0-2 | 5 |
| If a hit on an 0-2 count results in an RBI or a batter scoring later | 10 |
| Hitting a batter on an 0-2 count | 5 |
| Pitcher's failure to back up a play properly | 5 |
| Pitcher's failure to back up results in a run scored | 10 |
| Wild pitch that results in a run | 5 |
| Each additional wild pitch in same inning | 10 |
| Crossing up the catcher, resulting in a runner advancing | 5 |

# GAME PERFORMANCE EVALUATION FORMS

### Player Point Evaluation Form

| Positive | | Negative |
|---|---|---|
| | On base (except a fielder's choice) | |
| | Successful sacrifice | |
| | Score a run | |
| | RBI | |
| | Advance runner a base (other than a sacrifice) | |
| | Fine defensive play | |
| | Fine defensive play that saves a run | |
| | Alert, heads-up baserunning | |
| | Stolen base | |
| | Successful hit and run | |
| | Picking up signs or pitches | |
| | Pinch hit | |
| | Pinch RBI | |
| _____ | TOTAL | _____ |
| | Physical error that results in a run<br>Each additional run | |
| | Mental error that results in a run<br>Each additional run | |
| | Take a called third strike with runners in scoring position | |
| | Failure to advance a baserunner via a sacrifice | |
| | Baserunning error | |
| | Poor physical effort | |
| | Poor sportsmanship | |
| | Thrown out of a game | |
| | Mental error | |
| _____ | TOTAL | _____ |

## Pitching Point Evaluation Form

| Positive | | Negative |
|---|---|---|
| | Win a game | |
| | Save a game | |
| | Groundouts (11 or more in a seven-inning game) | |
| | No-hitter | |
| | One- or two-hitter | |
| | Throw 91 pitches in a seven-inning game | |
| | Two earned runs or less in a complete game | |
| | Two or less walks (seven-inning game) | |
| | Issue more than two walks but strikeout ratio is at least 2 to 1 | |
| | Complete game | |
| | Relief pitcher comes in with men on base and does not allow a run | |
| | Relief pitcher brought in to face tying or winning run without allowing to score | |
| | Outstanding relief job | |
| _____ | TOTAL | _____ |
| | Walk that results in run Additional walk that results in run same inning | |
| | Walk that forces a run | |
| | Walk after being ahead 0-2 | |
| | Giving up on a hit 0-2 (if hit results in RBI or batter later scores) | |
| | Hitting a batter on an 0-2 count | |
| | Pitcher failing to back up play | |
| | Wild pitch that results in a run (every other run in same inning) | |
| | Crossing up catcher, resulting in runner advancing | |
| _____ | TOTAL | _____ |

## Point System Totals

| Players' Names | Positive Points | Negative Points |
|---|---|---|
| 1. | | |
| 2. | | |
| 3. | | |
| 4. | | |
| 5. | | |
| 6. | | |
| 7. | | |
| 8. | | |
| 9. | | |
| 10. | | |
| 11. | | |
| 12. | | |
| 13. | | |
| 14. | | |
| 15. | | |
| 16. | | |
| 17. | | |
| 18. | | |

| Pitching Totals | Positive Points | Negative Points |
|---|---|---|
| 1. | | |
| 2. | | |
| 3. | | |
| 4. | | |

# INDEX